The tale of the mouse

The life and work of
Robert Thompson
the Mouseman of Kilburn

by Patricia Lennon

Foreword by Ian Thompson Cartwright

GREAT NORTHERN

First published in 2001 by
Great Northern Books
Midland Chambers, 1 Wells Road, Ilkley, West Yorkshire LS29 9JB
Tel: 01943 604027

© Patricia Lennon 2001

ISBN: 0-906899-88-5

Cover design Mark Pickthall
Designed by Blueprint Marketing Services Limited • Ilkley
Printed by Amadeus Press Ltd • Bradford

Photography from the collections of:

Blueprint Marketing Services Limited

David Joy

The National Trust Photographic Library

Robert Thompson Craftsmen Limited

The Star Inn, Harome/Cooper Bailey Photography

The Yorkshire Tourist Board

To BC whose idea it was and to my mother and children who went 'mouse-hunting' with me

The tale
of the mouse

Contents

General note

Many of the places included in these tours of the Mouseman's work are places of worship and are only open to the public at certain times. To avoid any disappointment, it is always advisable to phone ahead and check opening times.

Ian Thompson Cartwright (left) with Giles Thompson Cartwright (centre) and
Peter Cartwright (right) continue the tradition established by their Great
Grandfather, Robert Thompson. 1876 - 1955.

Foreword

by Ian Thompson Cartwright

As a small child, I would spend many hours in the workshop, making simple wooden boats to sail down the beck that runs through the village of Kilburn. I would listen to the craftsmen who had been trained by my Great Grandfather, Robert Thompson, talking about the outstanding jobs that they had worked on over the years. The pride I saw on their faces is repeated today when one of our craftsmen turns, stands back and views the item of furniture that he has just completed.

By following the tours listed within this book, you will be able to visit some of the sites where furniture produced by Great Grandfather and his craftsmen still stands as magnificently as the day it was installed. I like to imagine those craftsmen admiring their own skill and also, perhaps, a little surprised in realising just what they had created from a working drawing produced by their master, 'The Mouseman of Kilburn'.

Even today, I still experience a tremendous feeling of pride and joy when, visiting establishments such as Ampleforth College and York Minster, I discover an item of furniture that was made by my forefathers that I did not know was in existence.

The location of many of the churches and the countryside that you will pass through when following the 'Tale of the Mouse' really does show the North of England at its best. I personally have spent many a summer evening after a day in the workshop, driving along the country lanes, passing through the idyllic villages and admiring the views across the moors when covered in that beautiful purple heather carpet.

Should you be a 'mouse' collector or someone with an interest in Thompson furniture, I am certain you will enjoy viewing many of the previously unpublished family photographs that will provide you with an insight into the life and work of a very remarkable man, 'The Mouseman of Kilburn'.

Chapter one

ROBERT THOMPSON – EARLY YEARS AND INFLUENCES

Left: Robert Thompson.

Top: A view of Kilburn in Robert Thompson's day.

H andle a piece of Thompson furniture today and you are immediately in touch with the past. Each piece comprises layers of English history: the style and design will reflect the vision of a man born in the 19th century whose original inspiration came from ecclesiastical craftsmen of the Middle Ages. The history contained within that simple piece of furniture will unfold in this book - the story of Robert Thompson, the Mouseman of Kilburn.

It was a simple appreciation of craftsmanship and the natural beauties of English oak that inspired a young, country carpenter, at the start of the 20th century, to turn his back on the new innovations of mass production and instead rekindle the traditional wood carving techniques of a former age. Today, thousands of people across the world, inspired by the furniture he created, share the same appreciation of natural beauty and traditional skills. This is Robert Thompson's legacy.

The craftsman at work in his studio.

Robert Thompson as a young man outside his workshop, which is now the Visitor Centre in Kilburn.

The story starts in Kilburn, a picturesque village nestling in the Hambleton Hills, to the north of York. The village today is little different from the place where Robert Thompson was born in 1876 and where he lived for most of his life. The son of a local joiner, Robert Thompson was brought up in a small Elizabethan cottage in the centre of the village. The cottage eventually became his own home and today it remains the centre for the company he founded. Young Robert attended the local village school where he gained a good grounding in basic academic skills. At the age of 15, his father decided that Robert should learn a trade and, against the boy's wishes, arranged for him to serve an engineering apprenticeship with a firm in Cleckheaton, a busy town right at the smoking heart of West Yorkshire's industrial belt.

Robert later recorded his dismay at this drastic change of environment and described his years of apprenticeship as 'five years of penal servitude'. At the age of twenty, he persuaded his father to allow him to return to Kilburn and work with him in his joinery business. But the years in Cleckheaton were not entirely fruitless. During his apprenticeship, Robert's travels between home and his place of work took him through the city of Ripon with its imposing cathedral. Here he marvelled at the craftsmanship of the cathedral's mediaeval woodcarvings, particularly those of the master carver, William Bromflet. In later life, he spoke of this early experience as his inspiration to 'bring back to life the spirit of mediaeval oak work, which had been dead for so many long years'.

Back in Kilburn, as a young carpenter in his father's business, Robert Thompson's days were spent in mundane but essential repairs and construction of farm buildings. But the inspiration of Bromflet remained. Ideas and passion were slowly but very definitely being forged in the young man's heart and mind.

At the end of the 19th century, the work of a country tradesman was hard and the hours were long. However, Robert Thompson's drive was so great that what little free time he had from mending fences and building barns, he dedicated to learning more about the ancient craft of the mediaeval wood carvers: both the materials they used and the tools with which they worked. This early research led directly to the formation of his unique style of furniture -

English oak worked with an adze to produce a distinctive ripple surface effect. This combination of hard wearing, beautifully grained wood, complemented by the unusual adzed finish, was to become his signature, making his work easily identifiable with or without the presence of the later 'trademark' mouse.

During these formative years, whilst continuing his everyday trade as a country joiner, Robert also began to lay down supplies of oak for natural seasoning. Just as there were easier materials to work with than tough English oak, and contemporary tools were easier to handle than the mediaeval adze, so too, kiln drying offered a speedier means of seasoning wood prior to carving. Robert Thompson, perfectionist that he was, would have none of it. He believed that only natural seasoning could produce wood that would retain its beauty for decades even centuries. Thompson's approach was to saw whole trees lengthways into long

Robert (far right) and his craftsmen proudly display a finished church screen.

planks, in the early years with handsaws and later by machine. These were then stacked into piles, each plank separated by a small stick (a latt) and allowed to dry in the open air for up to five years.

It may appear that Robert Thompson's approach to his craft was almost perverse in adopting materials and techniques to make the task as laborious as possible. But it should be remembered that, to him, mass production was anathema: what truly mattered was to create a work of true craftsmanship that would stand the test of time. Apprentices recalled that he often encouraged them towards excellence by reminding them that their work would still be in use in 300 years' time. And his 'obsession' has been vindicated. Today, the company he founded continues to produce furniture, in English oak, seasoned in the same way, and using the same ancient tools and techniques that he revived - and the order book is full at least 12 months ahead.

However, back in Kilburn, at the dawn of the 20th century, Robert Thompson, then in his mid-twenties, could not possibly have realised how successful his vision would turn out to be. There remained the day-to-day necessity of earning a living, added to which was the cost of investing in oak for seasoning. To augment his carpentry work, he turned to stone masonry and several of his early gargoyles and First World War memorials exist in the villages around Kilburn. During the pre-First World War period, he also undertook his first ecclesiastical work - a pulpit for Yearsley church and altar rails for Harome.

The outbreak of the First World War brought turmoil and change to Kilburn as to all villages, towns and cities across the country. As the breadwinner of the family and a provider of local jobs and services, Robert Thompson was exempt from active duty. However, his workforce was dramatically reduced with many of his younger staff posted overseas as part of the war effort.

With the end of the human turmoil of the Great War, millions of people welcomed a return to the 'ordinary' lives they had known before 1914. But for Robert Thompson, events were about to take him on a very different track from that of the village carpenter. His ambition to rekindle 'the spirit of mediaeval oak work' was about to become reality.

Robert Thompson and his only daughter, Elsie, with one of his first ecclesiastical commissions, a pulpit for Yearsley Parish Church (1909).

Chapter two

THE HOUSE OF THE MOUSE

Picture courtesy of Ampleforth Abbey School

*Left: Father Paul Nevill,
Robert Thompson's first major patron.*

*Above: Mouse carving without front
paws.*

The turning point in Robert Thompson's career was a fortuitous meeting with Father Paul Nevill, a Catholic priest from Ampleforth College. In conversation with one of his parishioners, Sydney Mawe, Father Paul outlined his plans to erect a large crucifix in the cemetery at Ampleforth but explained that he was having difficulty in locating a carpenter with a piece of oak large enough to carry out the project. Sydney Mawe introduced him to his neighbour, Robert Thompson, and the contract was confirmed.

That was the start of a long-lasting friendship between both men and a working relationship between the College and Robert Thompson's company that remains alive today. And yet, were it not for the craftsman's optimism and pragmatism, that opportunity may have been missed, as he revealed later in life:

'I said "Yes" to Father Paul without hesitation knowing I hadn't the oak and I didn't know where it was coming from but I wasn't going to say "no"'.

It was also around this time that Thompson introduced his famous trademark: a mouse carved in relief into every piece of work. No one knows exactly when or where he carved his first mouse but an extract from a letter in 1949 to the Reverend John Fisher allows Robert Thompson to explain its creation in his own words:

'The origin of the mouse as my mark was almost in the way of being an accident. I and another carver were carving a huge cornice for a screen and he happened to say something about being as poor as a church mouse. I said I'll carve a mouse here and did so, then it struck me what a lovely trade mark. This is about 30 years ago'.

Later to his grandsons, who continued his work, he explained how he was humoured by the thought of a mouse scraping and chewing its way through the hardest wood, working away quietly while nobody takes any notice. He saw an immediate parallel with his own workshop, hidden away in the Hambleton Hills and so also was born his motto, 'industry in quiet places'.

This staircase completed by Robert Thompson in 1924 for Upsall Castle is 'pre-mouse'. It is said that Robert Thompson offered at a later date to 'sign' the work by adding his famous mouse. The owner declined, arguing that a piece by the Mouseman without the tell-tale mouse would have greater rarity value!

13

14

Above: Kilburn workshop c1925.

Inset: Conditions and working practice
remain similar today.

The inclusion and, indeed, the style of mouse carved on early Thompson furniture provide a clue to the age of the piece. Pieces carved before (approximately) 1920 do not include the mouse carving. Between circa 1920 and 1930, the mouse was carved with front paws, which disappeared after that date being too prone to damage. The style of mouse often also indicates the particular craftsman for each piece. Apprentice carvers were only considered to be fully trained once they could carve the mouse to their master's exacting standards.

The mouse, created as a whimsy, has become a lasting and distinctive trademark - probably one of the earliest 'logos' created in the 20th century to still be around, unchanged, today. However, Robert Thompson never let the distinctive little symbol dominate his work. It is usually tucked away in unobtrusive corners, providing a special challenge to those who seek it out in dimly lit church interiors.

From that first commission at Ampleforth, Robert Thompson's reputation rapidly spread. Over the next 35 years, the Thompson mouse was to find a wide range of homes across the British Isles and farther afield, from small country churches to Westminster Abbey; academic institutions to town halls; corporate headquarters to country hotels; and in the private homes of individuals who appreciated the quality and craftsmanship that Robert Thompson and his workers brought to every piece.

Crucifix at Ampleforth, 1919.

As commissions started to increase, so too did the number of craftsmen and apprentices at the tiny workshop in Kilburn, reaching a total workforce of about 35 men and boys at the time of Robert Thompson's death.

While the mouse travelled far and wide, its creator, Robert Thompson, stayed firmly rooted in his home village of Kilburn. He married a local girl, lived and worked in the same cottage where he had spent his childhood and where he, in turn, brought up his only child, Elsie.

In 1955, he died and was buried in the small church graveyard in Kilburn where a simple tombstone marks his grave. His real and lasting monument is just a stone's throw away at the House of the Mouse - the workshop he founded and which today continues the traditional skills of wood carving that he revived and made his own.

Top right: Robert Thompson (with stick) outside his Kilburn home which is now the company's offices and showroom.

Inset right: The Mouseman cottage today.

Top left: Robert Thompson and his dogs, Ling and Snipe.

Left: Robert Thompson, looking slightly uncomfortable, in a studio portrait with his daughter Elsie.

Far left: Fine clothes for the country craftsman on his wedding day. The local newspaper described his bride, Ada, as 'attired in a dress of grey silk trimmed with chiffon and chiffon hat to match; she carried a bouquet composed of lilies of the valley and maiden hair fern.' The couple were reported to have taken their honeymoon in Goole.

Left: Craftsmen at work seen from the visitors' viewing gallery in the workshop.

Chapter three

THE MOUSEMAN LEGACY LIVES ON – KILBURN TODAY

Stacks of oak outside the Mouseman Visitors' Centre in Kilburn village centre.

Visitors to Kilburn today will find it little changed in appearance from Robert Thompson's time: a huddle of cottages, either side of a brook, define the main street. The whole scene conforms to the image of a typical sleepy English village. It is the kind of place in which the casual visitor may imagine nothing much happens. And yet from here items of furniture are despatched to the far most corners of the globe. Indeed, aficionados of Thompson's work travel from across the world to visit his birthplace. Their travels are rewarded as the village and its surrounding countryside offer much for 'mouse' enthusiasts.

The Mouseman Visitor Centre presents a fascinating history of Robert Thompson, and includes replicas of the interiors of his cottage and workshop, complete with original examples of furniture carved by the master himself. Also included are exquisite hand-coloured designs for furniture and room settings. Equally fascinating are the order books and ledgers on display which record early customers' requirements and the prices paid - chairs at 30 shillings each and tables at £16 represented a sound investment for Ampleforth College in 1936.

The workshop at Kilburn has been featured on many TV programmes, including Blue Peter and Harry Secombe's Highways. The BBC's Antiques Roadshow programme (pictured during filming) confirmed the collectable status of Thompson furniture - the antiques of tomorrow.

The Visitor Centre is also a focus for living history as visitors may observe craftsmen at work, demonstrating the type of tools, techniques and skills that Robert Thompson practised. The craftsmen are happy to provide a commentary as they work, explaining the origins of a particular design or the technique being used. Visitors may also be able to try their hand at adzing and will quickly appreciate the skill required.

Directly opposite the Visitor Centre are the current showrooms and workshops. The range of domestic furniture produced in the Kilburn workshop today includes many pieces that remain true to Robert Thompson's original designs. As in the earliest days of the company, ecclesiastical work and civic commissions are an important element of the business. In fact, the links with Robert Thompson's original work are never far away: original books on mediaeval carvings, which provided inspiration for Robert Thompson, are still used today for reference in new commissioned pieces.

Picture courtesy of Neale's Auctioneers.

Pre-war 'mouse' furniture commands high prices today. This 1930's dining table fetched about £20,000 at auction in early 2001, the same price as a good Georgian Regency mahogany triple pillar table.

19

Below and right: Craftsmen at work.

On receiving a new commission, the designer will research where the piece is to be placed and formulate designs for the client's approval. A working drawing will then be produced along with a cutting list, which will stipulate the amount and type of timber required. If the piece is to become part of a standard range of furniture, a prototype will then be produced. Once full approval has been given to the design, it is then passed onto one of the company's 30 or so craftsmen who will bring the piece to life.

Not only the designs but also the actual production processes are little changed from Robert Thompson's days. At the company's workshop, a special viewing gallery allows visitors to observe the craftsman at work on the actual production of pieces of furniture.

The starting point for any piece of Thompson furniture will typically begin in a field or forest, many years before the actual carving process begins. The company sources oak from across the country, preferring wood that has grown in the north of England and purchasing between 200 and 500 felled oak trees every year. Visitors to Kilburn will see huge stacks of sawn English oak, being stored and seasoned in the open air, in the traditional way. At any one time there is more than five years' worth of oak in storage.

Stack of sawn oak being delivered to the workshop - a familiar sight in Kilburn village.

Inset: Skilled use of the adze carves scallops of oak to create the familiar ripple-effect surface.

Each tree is personally inspected before purchase and the age of the tree is calculated. Damage to a tree suffered many years previously from frost or pest can show up as 'ring shake' or 'star shake', which detract from the appearance of the grain. Lightning strikes will result in the timber not taking colour during the fuming process. As Thompson furniture is not stained or painted, it is impossible to hide such defects in the finished piece of furniture.

Each piece of Thompson furniture is taken from start to finish by one craftsman. All the craftsmen - and they range in age from 20-year-olds to septuagenarians - joined the company from school and have been trained in-house. They serve a four- or five-year apprenticeship, working under different carvers so that they experience a range of approaches and styles. This ensures that each craftsman finds scope for the expression of his own personal style within the overall guidelines of the Thompson approach.

The in-house training and apprenticeship system leads to smooth transfer of skills and maintains a direct line from today's craftsmen back to Robert Thompson himself.

When starting a particular job, whether a piece from the current range or a specially commissioned piece, the craftsman responsible will personally select the timber. He will look for specific qualities of grain or colour that will enhance the design in question and also ensure that the timber selected has been seasoned correctly. Wood for a tabletop, which will typically be two inches thick, will have been seasoned outside for a minimum of four years.

Having selected the appropriate timber, the craftsman will then carry out rough cutting to shape. The piece proceeds to the bench, where the actual carving and assembling will take place. The length of time spent at this stage will depend on the piece in question: typically, a dining chair will take 20 hours of bench time; a bureau may take four weeks.

It is at this stage that the adzing process takes place, which gives the surface of Thompson furniture its distinctive rippled appearance. The craftsman first marks out in pencil the lines that the adze will follow, matching the direction of the grain on the surface of the wood. The piece of timber is placed on the floor and the craftsman stands on top of it. With a gentle pendulum motion, he swings the adze slowly between his legs, slicing slivers of wood from the surface.

Seeing the adze used in this way, alongside heavy boots and hard hands, to produce a soft rippled surface, demonstrates the supreme skill of the master. After adzing, the wood is sanded by hand and then placed in the fuming chamber, which is filled with ammonia vapour. The alkali in the ammonia reacts with the acid in the oak to impart a soft honey colour on the surface of the oak. This method of colouring oak was used in the Middle Ages, using urine instead of ammonia. The fuming process was employed by Robert Thompson in preference to the staining and dying processes more prevalent in the early 19th century.

Generally taking 24 hours, the fuming time can be varied according to a customer's preference for a particular hue. The eventual results are affected by various factors including the age and condition of the wood and even the outside weather. Once again, the idiosyncratic nature of the process ensures that each piece of Mouseman furniture is unique.

Once the fuming process is complete, the craftsman will apply a wax paste by brush to the surface of the wood, which is then polished by hand. If the surface is likely to be exposed to moisture, a polyurethene varnish is used.

The actual assembly of a piece of furniture also follows a centuries old tradition. All mortise and tenon joints are doweled for strength and stability using oak dowels, which each craftsman makes himself as part of the whole production process.

Altar inside Kilburn church.

The final stage in the production process is the upholstery. Chair seats are webbed with cotton and finished with Connolly leather. The link between the Thompson and Connolly companies goes back to Robert Thompson's early days. He selected Connolly leather as he believed the oak, russet hide and wrought iron fixings produced a particularly pleasing aesthetic combination.

On leaving the Mouseman Visitor Centre and showroom, 'mouse' enthusiasts may be interested to visit St Mary's church in Kilburn. Here they will find early examples of Thompson's work and that of his successors, including an unusual set of oak headstones in the graveyard. Inside the church are a 'breeches' bible showcase, a litany desk, lectern and traceried pulpit, all bearing the discreet but distinctive mouse trademark. Note also on the lectern a carved lizard indicating this as a piece designed by the architect Ernest Walker, whose family crest featured a lizard. Similar 'mouse' and 'lizard' work can be found in St Luke's church in York. In 1958, the chapel of St Thomas at Kilburn was refurbished as a memorial to Robert Thompson, the company's craftsmen producing all the chapel's furnishing in the distinctive adzed style. To sit within the cool stillness of this ancient chapel, surrounded by beautiful hand-crafted oak, allows the visitor to contemplate, and perhaps share, the quiet passion that motivated Robert Thompson.

Whilst in Kilburn, visitors can combine their quest for the mouse with a search for refreshment at the Forresters Arms. Not surprisingly, being situated next to Thompson's workshop, this delightful village inn is overrun with 'mice' of the wooden variety.

*Kilburn church, and the grave
yard. In the foreground is
Robert Thompson's final resting
place. The company's workshop is
seen behind the church.*

Chapter four

Around Kilburn (20 miles)

Coxwold

First stop for many 'mouse seekers' on leaving Kilburn is the nearby village of Coxwold. On entering the village, visitors cannot miss the church of St Michael, which, with its unusual

St Michael's church, Coxwold.

octagonal tower, dominates the wide main street. The church was built between 1420 and 1430 and is considered to be one of the best examples of perpendicular architecture in the former North Riding. Inside are numerous fascinating historical and architectural features: the 18th century box pews were originally rented by local families and were introduced by the parson, Laurence Sterne (of whom, more later); 14th century stained glass in the north nave windows is older than the church itself having been brought from an earlier Norman church; the Royal coat of arms of George II over the chancel arch was introduced to act as a reminder to worshippers that the church belonged to the King rather than the Roman Pope; and superb early 17th, 18th and 19th century monuments trace the history of the local Belayse family.

The reading stand at St Michael's church, Coxwold - a collaboration between Joseph Heu and Robert Thompson.

St Michael's church, interior.

For lovers of Mouseman furniture, the church is best known as home to an interesting collaborative work between Robert Thompson and an Austrian wood carver, Joseph Heu. In 1941, fleeing from anti-Semitic persecution, Joseph Heu was given refuge and employment by Robert Thompson. Their mutual respect for each other's work came to fruition in a commission for a new lectern at Coxwold church. Robert Thompson carved the pedestal (note the mouse on the base) whilst his Austrian friend and colleague completed the reading desk. Later, Joseph paid a special tribute to his Yorkshire mentor with a carved bas-relief portrait of Robert Thompson (complete with a renegade mouse creeping into his sleeve) that today can be viewed in the museum in Kilburn.

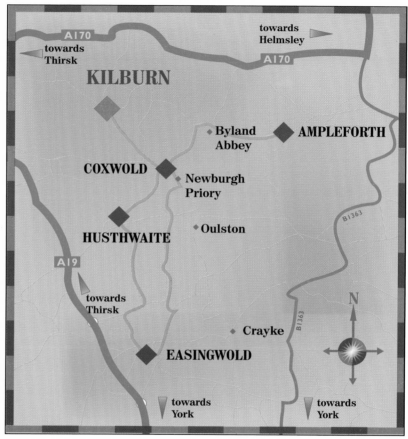

Thompson mice are also evident here in the Lady Chapel, hiding on the simple oak altar and under the ledge of the niche in the wall. A further mouse is to be found on the Bible case, which contains a 'Breeches Bible', printed in 1601. The mice at St Michael's are in good company, as the roof within the church contains some fine examples of mediaeval roof bosses carved with various birds and beasts.

In the church porch is the tombstone of Laurence Sterne, the 18th century author of *Tristram Shandy* and *A Sentimental Journey*, who was vicar at Coxwold from 1760 to 1768. The tombstone was erected in London on

Sterne's death in 1768 by a group of Masons. It was removed to Coxwold in 1969 when Sterne's body was re-interred here. His grave is now sited by the south wall of the nave just outside the porch.

The former vicarage, Shandy Hall, is located near the church on the road to Kilburn. It has been painstakingly restored by the Laurence Sterne Trust and provides a step back in time to the days when the amusing parson - who entertained 18th century London society and was a friend of Hogarth, Garrick and Reynolds - lived quietly there. The house is open to the public and is well worth a visit.

Before leaving the village, visitors may wish to seek refreshment at the Fauconberg Arms, which contains many examples of work by Thompson and his successors. At the village crossroads, the road signs point to the next destination on the Mouse tour, Husthwaite.

Husthwaite

A pleasant drive of just two miles down winding country lanes brings us to Husthwaite. On entering the village turn right into the High Street where St Nicholas' church is found opposite the village green. An original Norman church with later additions, the oak roof was one of Robert Thompson's earliest commissions. Other Mouseman work includes a beautiful traceried altar, lectern, litany desk and reredos. Follow the signs from the village green to Easingwold.

A roadside view of the lake at Newburgh Priory near Coxwold.

Easingwold

On entry, the little market town of Easingwold may at first appear unprepossessing but first impressions are deceptive. Following the signs for the market square leads one into a charming cobbled market place, surrounded by 18th and 19th century

Husthwaite church.

houses and shops. Driving out of the square and uphill, turn left into Church Hill. Following this road for a few hundred yards, the church of All Saints and St John appears on the right, with its car park opposite.

Described by Nicholas Pevsner as a 'typical North Country church, dark, grey, low and long and without battlements or parapet', this unremarkable exterior hides some fine examples of Mouseman work. Visitors will need to look closely to define the mouse hiding on the High Altar (from 1948) and the Lady Chapel altar. Other Thompson pieces include the reredos behind the high altar, the parclose screen dividing the Lady Chapel from the nave and a credence table.

Turning back down Church Hill towards the junction with Easingwold's main street, proceed straight ahead past pretty cottages and turn left at the next junction. This circular and very scenic route leads past Newburgh Priory on the return to Coxwold. Arriving back at Coxwold, take the road to Ampleforth which passes stunning Byland Abbey.

Stained glass window at Easingwold church.

29

Byland Abbey, between Coxwold and Ampleforth.

Ampleforth

For Mouseman enthusiasts, Ampleforth - the Benedictine monastery and school - is a mecca not to be missed. As we have seen, it played a pivotal role in the career of Robert Thompson. From that first commission of a crucifix, for Father Paul Nevill, extended a personal involvement for Robert Thompson, which lasted for 31 years until his death. Ampleforth contains extensive examples of work by Robert Thompson, including his *piece de resistance*, the library, which he always referred to as 'my room'. His work in the library, started in 1934 with bookcases, carrels (private study desks), chairs, tables and even waste bins. In 1950, he added the immense door. A table in the library bears the inscription 'VPN from RT', testament to his longstanding friendship with Father Paul. However, as it is a busy school, only the works in the Abbey Church are available for viewing by the public and only by prior arrangement.

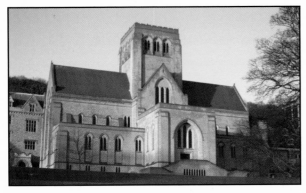

Ampleforth Abbey church.

The work in the Abbey dates from 1928 and represents Robert Thompson's first commission for Sir Giles Gilbert Scott,

Robert Thompson's ledger for 1936 indicates the diverse range of pieces produced for Ampleforth and the prices charged.

one of the most renowned architects of the early 20th century, whose output ranged from the Anglian cathedral in Liverpool to Bankside Powerstation (now Tate Modern) and the classic red telephone box. Robert Thompson was justly proud of the Abbot's choir stall. On being asked by Sir Giles where he was thinking of making the joins, Robert is reported to have replied: 'Why do you want a join? If you come to me, you can have it in one piece'.

In 1955, Robert Thompson's last and poignant commission at the school was a plaque to commemorate Old Boys who had perished in the Second World War. Today, the workshop at Kilburn continues to carry out commissions for the school and monastery, maintaining the relationship that commenced between Father Nevill and Robert Thompson so long ago.

Arrangements to visit Ampleforth Abbey church should be made in advance through the Hospitality and Pastoral Service Office, telephone 01439 766889. Donations are welcomed.

A candle-lit view of a side chapel in the Abbey church.

The choir stalls at Ampleforth Abbey church - the first of Robert Thompson's successful collaborations with the eminent architect, Sir Giles Gilbert Scott.

The centrepiece of Mouseman work at Ampleforth College is the library, which Robert Thompson called 'my room'. Perhaps to provide some light relief for the boys studying within the library's private study carrels, Thompson thoughtfully incorporated humourous touches such as comical dragons, laughing heads and, of course, the Kilburn mouse. The mouse here is particularly pleasing, chasing his own tail in a never-ending circle.

Chapter five

Lower Ryedale (50 miles)

Helmsley Castle.

Yorkshire Tourist Board

This 50-mile round trip through beautiful Ryedale countryside takes in some fine examples of Robert Thompson's work in both ecclesiastical and secular surroundings. It also provides opportunity for detours to stunning Rievaulx Abbey and Helmsley Castle.

Helmsley

The little market town of Helmsley nestles among surrounding hills and is bordered by the River Rye. It is the administrative home of the North York Moors National Park and is a popular stopping-off point for visitors to the area. Red-roofed houses, shops and wide streets surround the market square where a fine ancient cross contrasts with a Victorian obelisk designed by the eminent architect Sir George Gilbert Scott, whose other works include the Albert Memorial and St Pancras Station in London (as well as St Mary's church in Ambleside, which features in the Lake District 'mouse' tour).

The church of All Saints stands just behind the market square. The lower part of its tower is 13th century whilst the south doorway and chancel arch both bear distinctive Norman zigzag carvings. Look out also for the 11th century hogback stone in the porch.

Inside the church, funerary monuments, stained glass and various historical artifacts provide interest for visitors. Thompson enthusiasts will, however, head straight to the sanctuary where the panelling commemorates those members of the XXII Dragoons who were killed in the Normandy campaigns of 1944/45. The panelling was commissioned by

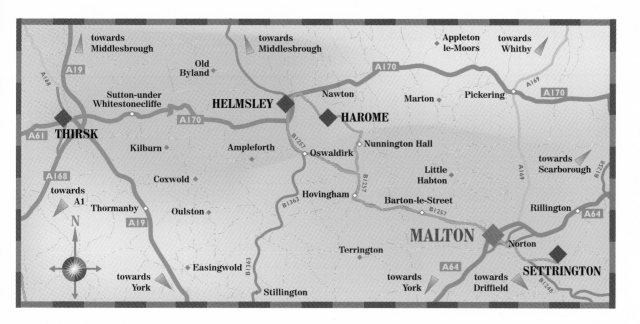

Major Clifford who, with his squadron, was based near Kilburn after the Dunkirk campaign. There he came across Robert Thompson and was so fascinated by the craftsman's skills that he ordered several pieces of furniture for his own home, Frampton Court, a 15th century manor house in Gloucestershire. Major Clifford felt obliged to mention to Thompson that his prices were extremely low and that he could charge more if they were sold in London. The craftsman simply replied that he knew he could get more in London but that he preferred to

work in his home county, making furniture to order, so that he knew where each piece was going. Also note the altar rails' distinct adzed finish. Inscribed to Walter Baldwin 'people's warden' who died in 1926, the mouse runs up the rail post.

Leaving the church, it is just a short walk straight ahead, then turning right opposite the small bridge to the spectacular remains of Helmsley castle, which dates back to around 1200 AD. The remains of a double ditch and the bridge that crossed it can clearly be

seen, as can later developments, including two barbicans from the mid 13th century, a 14th century kitchen and 15th century buttery. Elizabethan additions include a fine plaster ceiling and frieze, panelling and an oak fireplace.

The castle started to decline in the late 17th century following its purchase by the Duncombe family and their commissioning of a new building, Duncombe House, the design of which was carried out under the instruction of Sir John Vanburgh.

The landscaped haven of Duncombe Park, complete with temples and terraces, commands superb views of Rievaulx Abbey and Helmsley Castle. Equally stunning views may be obtained from Rievaulx Terrace, a swathe of green nearly half a mile long with temples at each end. The Terrace is now owned by the National Trust.

Just over two miles north of Helmsley lies Rievaulx Abbey, the earliest Cistercian abbey in Yorkshire. For many people, the beauty of its setting leaves it rivalled only by Tintern Abbey on the Wye. Visited on a fine summer's day, few would disagree.

Old Malton

Leaving Helmsley, take the B1257 road towards Malton. Just north of Hovingham is the 16th century manor house, Nunnington Hall, now owned by the National Trust and open to the public. Arriving in Old Malton, the church of St Mary is located in the centre of the village. Under the west window a carved oak door with

The North York Moors (Rosedale).

Litany desk for Settrington church, photographed by Robert Thompson prior to installation.

traceried panels by Thompson is in complete harmony with the 12th century doorway that contains it. On the altar, the pulpit and lectern also bear distinctive Thompson carving and the sign of the mouse. From Malton, follow the B1248 Driffield Road for two miles before turning left for Settrington.

Settrington

The picturesque village of Settrington comprises a cluster of red-roofed houses around the sturdy, buttressed

34

15th century church of All Saints. Inside the church, the litany desk and organ seat are particularly fine examples of Robert Thompson's work. There are numerous other architectural features both inside and outside the church which will tempt the visitor to linger a while. Look out particularly for the 12th century font and, outside, at the 13th century zigzag and floral carvings over the south doorway arch. Casting an eye skywards to the top of the tower reveals some interesting carved heads and an unusual kneeling figure with a man behind.

Harome

From Settrington, retrace your steps to Malton and Hovingham, from there follow signposts to Nunnington and Harome. Here the Star Inn not only provides a pleasant opportunity for refreshment but also contains some attractive pieces of Thompson furniture.

Suitably refreshed, visitors now have only a short drive back to Helmsley.

Picture by Paul Cooper of Cooper Bailey Photography, courtesy of The Star Inn, Harome.

Star Inn, Harome.

35

Chapter six

East Yorkshire (70 miles)

Beverley Minster.

Yorkshire Tourist Board

This 70-mile journey offers something for everyone: the busy shops and architectural heritage of Beverley; the gentle scenery of the Wolds and the bracing sea air of Bridlington.

Beverley

In terms of ecclesiastical heritage and Thompson's art, the small town of Beverley has an embarrassment of riches. In the 1940s, Arthur Mee, in his review of *The King's England,* described the town as 'an exquisite beauty, unsurpassed in Yorkshire. York Minster is not more lovely than Beverley Minster, and as if that were not enough for a small town, here is the beautiful church of St Mary to keep it company'. Both churches are also central to this Thompson tour and the work in each commemorates the fallen of the 1939-45 war.

At the Minster, which is considered to be one of the finest Gothic buildings in Europe, Thompson's work is to be found within the Military Chapel. Here the altar rails, chairs, entrance screen, Book of Remembrance and the door to the staircase are all fine examples of Mouseman work. Each of the chairs is dedicated to a fallen soldier and all bear the mouse in silent witness. Those wishing to complete this particular Mouseman tour in one day will have little time to linger within the Minster although it would be a shame to miss the choir with its unique misericords. This brief encounter will no doubt persuade many to return another day to do full justice to the truly impressive interior.

The short walk from the Minster to St Mary's allows visitors to take in some of the sights of this charming town. The narrow streets reveal a hotchpotch of architectural styles, all contained within the remains of an ancient ditch and a palisade with five gates, one of which, the North Bar dating from 1409, has been restored.

At St Mary's, the oak door acts as a war memorial. Designed by the architect, Leslie Temple Moore, it was commissioned during Robert Thompson's lifetime but was completed after his death by his grandsons. The panels bear the names of fallen parishioners. The mouse may be seen lurking at the right-hand base of the door.

Whilst in the church, look out for another animal of interest - a statue of a hare dressed in man's clothes - it is said to have provided Lewis Carroll with his inspiration for the White Rabbit in *Alice in Wonderland*.

To take in all the sights that Beverley has to offer would easily occupy a full day but Bridlington and the sea beckon.

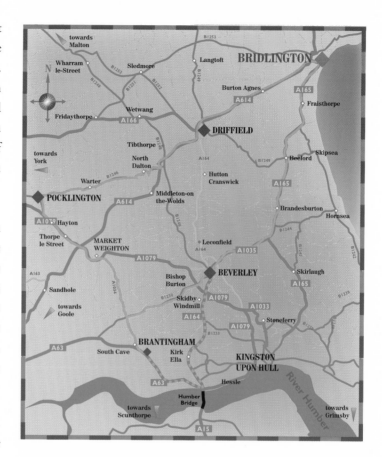

Bridlington

Leaving Beverley on the A1035 road, it is a 20-mile journey north east to Bridlington or 'Brid' as it is popularly known: and Bridlington *is* popular. Its heyday, like so many other English seaside towns, may have passed but Bridlington still offers much for lovers of the sea. The South Bay has a particularly fine stretch of sand for bathers and offers all the usual seaside family attractions. The picturesque quay by the waterfront is linked to the original Old Town inland by a stretch of Victorian buildings which followed the coming of the railway to cater for the new wave of Victorian holiday makers. The town is rich in maritime

Beverley War Memorial.

Bench end in Bridlington Priory church by Robert Thompson. He was honoured to be asked by the Priory to make exact reproductions of mediaeval stalls, which were originally carved in 1519 by his 'hero' William Bromflet. The originals were removed to another church.

Bridlington.

history - it was here that the ship carrying Charles Stuart's queen sought refuge from the pursuing Roundheads - and aeronautical history too, with the interesting Amy Johnson Collection at nearby Sewerby Hall. So there is much to detain visitors in Bridlington but, for Mouseman enthusiasts, the focus of the visit is the Priory Church of St Mary the Virgin in the Old Town.

The church is all that remains of a great Augustinian monastery founded at the beginning of the 12th century by Walter de Gant. Following the dissolution of the monasteries under Henry VIII, the nave was all that was allowed to remain standing. This too eventually fell into ruin until it was restored in the 1870s by Sir George Gilbert Scott.

St Mary's has many superb examples of Robert Thompson's work including two stalls in the chancel. These bear exact reproductions of carvings made in 1519 by William Bromflet of Ripon, the mediaeval master wood carver whose work in Ripon Cathedral provided the young Robert Thompson with his original creative inspiration.

Other late Thompson work within St Mary's includes the war memorial screens (another design by Leslie Temple Moore), the font canopy (1955) and the parclose screen gates to the sanctuary (1949). The pulpit panelling, canopy and spiral staircase were added in 1960 to a much older stone pulpit. The Thompson carving is highly ornate, including representations of Viking ships and scenes from the life of Christ. Other smaller items are also found here, including a sanctuary chair and prie-dieu (kneeling prayer desk), a table at the west end of the church and a lectern stool. In the Bayle Gate Upper Room are a number of large, adzed refrectory tables.

Leaving the sea, the Mouseman trail now follows the A614 past Driffield and then the B1246 across the Wolds to Pocklington.

View of Skidby Windmill

Pocklington

Coming down from the Wolds, Pocklington appears on the plain below - a picturesque market town with an imposing mediaeval church at its centre. The village was the home of the 18th century anti-slavery campaigner, William Wilberforce, who was educated in the old grammar school here. The church, known as the 'cathedral of the Wolds', has Norman foundations, a few elements of which remain including a font bowl. However, the major part of the church, including the imposing tower, comprises 15th century additions. There are fascinating carvings of gargoyles and men's faces both inside and outside the church. Here, visitors can literally play 'cat and mouse' by seeking out the Norman carving of a cat's head in the porch and Thompson's trademark rodent on the altar rails. Leaving Pocklington on the Market Weighton road (the A1079), the nearby gardens of Burnby Hall offer an attractive diversion especially for lovers of water lilies - the gardens are renowned for their lily ponds.

Go past Market Weighton and then take the A1034 South Cave road to Brantingham.

Brantingham

At the church in this small village, Thompson's work is represented by two unusual wooden crosses in the churchyard, which commemorate members of the Massey family. The mouse may be found on each cross.

The church combines a mediaeval tower with Norman foundations. The south doorway is 12th century and the interesting font inside is only slightly younger.

Retrace your route through South Cave, from where it is only 10 miles back to Beverley via the B1230.

Alternatively, follow the A63 towards the Humber Bridge and then the A164 back to Beverly, passing Skidby Windmill along the way. Built in 1821, Skidby is the last working windmill north of the Humber. It is open to the public at weekends and Wednesday to Sunday in the summer.

Chapter seven

Ainsty Country (35 Miles)

Bishopthorpe Palace.

The city of York provides an excellent starting and finishing point for this short tour which, in a 35-mile round trip, reveals some hidden gems of Mouseman carvings. The tour allows visitors to explore quiet backwater villages, which are so often overlooked by drivers speeding along the busy A64 to and from York.

Bishopthorpe

The village of Bishopthorpe lies just two miles south of York close to the famous racecourse. On first entering the village, it appears quiet and unassuming and it is something of a shock, therefore, to come across Bishopthorpe Palace, the present home of the Archbishop of York. The Palace is not open to the public but the view from the entrance gate of the main building, fronted by manicured lawns, presents an idyllic picture.

The church of St Andrew is just across the road from the Palace. The pale stonework of the church is half covered in ivy and creepers and, in summer, is framed all around by a border of 'cottage garden' flowers. Visitors may rest awhile on benches thoughtfully provided to allow one to soak up the atmosphere of this almost perfect English village church.

Inside the church, the work of Robert Thompson is immediately presented in the form of the magnificent, eight-sided, pinnacled font cover. Designed by GG Pace, it is suspended over the ancient stone font, which was transferred to the church, along with the two church bells, from the much older church of St Crux in York.

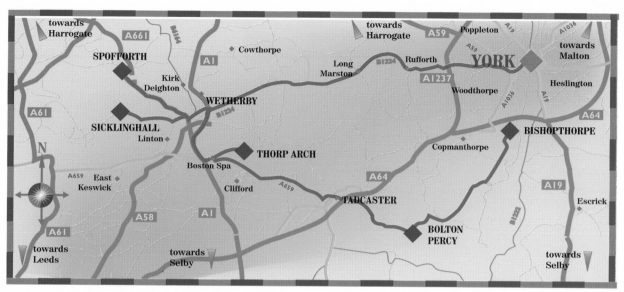

The carved mouse appears immediately above the start of the inscription to Augusta Anne Maclaglan, a faithful worshipper in the church, who died in 1908.

Whilst in the church, take time to view the stained glass windows which depict interesting scenes from the village's history, including Archbishop de Gray repealing the Game Law in 1226 and King Charles I's visit of 1633. One of the most loved windows is the 'school window' which was presented in memory of a former school teacher. It depicts four class room scenes from 1350, 1693, 1846 and, finally, 1950.

On leaving the church, take a walk on past the Palace and then turn left down Chantry Lane. This leads to the riverside and the site of the former parish church of St Andrew, now marked by a stone cross where the altar once stood. Ancient tombs from the graveyard are stacked against the wall and make fascinating reading. Past the riverbank comes a constant stream of pleasure craft and tourist cruisers, on their way to and from the city of York.

Bolton Percy

Returning to the car, follow the road signs to Copmanthorpe and Bolton Percy. Bolton Percy is reached in five miles.

The church which dates from the early 15th century is a fine example of the perpendicular style. It dominates the village green and is indicative of the former importance of the village as a trading centre and river thoroughfare.

Robert Thompson carved the lych gate which bears an inscription of Samuel Smith of Oxton Hall who died in 1927. A well-worn figure of St Oswald guards the entrance to the lych gate. Visitors may spend some time looking for the Thompson mouse as it is not easy to find. For those who fail to locate the mouse, its position is noted at the end of this chapter.

The lych gate for Bolton Percy church assembled outside Thompson's workshop prior to installation.

The interior of this church is fascinating; the box pews are Jacobean as is the smaller of the two pulpits; the larger pulpit is Caroline. The East window above the altar is also of interest, being the only remaining mediaeval glass in which Mary, the Blessed Virgin, is prominent.

Mousework is manifest in the altar rails. These are very plain and are not in the usual obviously adzed finish. The mouse symbol is found inset on the inside of the left-hand altar rail as one looks at the altar. The mouse also appears creeping along the edge of the hymn number box. Two standard candle sticks, dedicated to HS Woolcombe are no longer on the altar but are kept inside the vestry.

On leaving the church, cross the road to the side of the church and enter the cemetery garden through an iron gate. Inside this walled garden is a riotous tumult of flowers in the summer almost obscuring the tombstones within.

Before leaving the village, a walk round to the other side of the church leads to the Crown Inn. A pleasant garden leads down to the river, which is crossed by a narrow wooden footbridge.

Thorp Arch

On leaving Bolton Percy, follow the signs for Tadcaster, there turn right in

View from the bridge at Boston Spa.

the town centre to take the A659 towards Wetherby through Boston Spa. In the centre of Boston Spa, turn right following the sign for the British Library, crossing the arched stone bridge over the wide river. Travelling up the hill, the church of All Saints appears on the right after a couple of hundred yards. The church is usually locked, so it may be advisable to phone ahead.

Inside the church, all the woodwork is by Thompson apart from the altar which comes from the Austrian town of Oberammergau, famous for its mediaeval passion play. The majority of the Thompson work here dates from 1935 and was considered by Thompson to be among his best work, notably the pulpit, two carved screens and pews.

Whilst the honey coloured stone houses of Thorp Arch present a pretty picture, there is little else in the village to detain the visitor and so retrace the route back to Boston Spa village and then follow the signs for Wetherby and on to Sicklinghall.

Sicklinghall

Entering the village of Sicklinghall, travel up the hill, which forms the main street and the catholic church of Mary Immaculate is found on the left. Inside, mice are to be found everywhere; on the pews, the tables at the back of church, the altar rails, panelling and screen. Even the Stations of the Cross are the work of

Sicklinghall church.

the Mouseman. The church continues to purchase Thompson furniture, some of its latest pieces include a Pascal candlestick in memoriam of Reginald Morton Holmes (1998) who was a great supporter of the church and a lover of Mouseman furniture.

Spofforth

From Sicklinghall, retrace the route back to the outskirts of Wetherby and turn sharp left onto the A661 for Spofforth. Here the church of All Hallows contains one of Robert

Thompson's last works, a board recording the names of the church's rectors. Other Thompson pieces include the lectern, rector's stall, choir stall and altar rails.

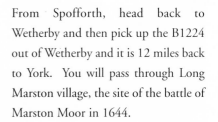
Spofforth Castle, close to the centre of the village, is open to the public.

Whilst in the churchyard, look out for the grave of John Metcalfe, otherwise known as 'Blind Jack of Knaresborough' who despite losing his sight as a small boy, built up a national reputation as a roadmaker.

From Spofforth, head back to Wetherby and then pick up the B1224 out of Wetherby and it is 12 miles back to York. You will pass through Long Marston village, the site of the battle of Marston Moor in 1644.

The hidden mouse on the lych gate at Bolton Percy church can be found on the outside left, when facing the church.

Chapter eight

Lower Wharfedale
(35 Miles)

Yorkshire Tourist Board

Harrogate.

The busy towns of Harrogate and Ilkley are ideal starting and finishing points for this circular tour. Both are well equipped with shops, refreshment places, museums and natural beauty to ensure that this short tour provides a full and varied day's amusement for the most discerning visitor. For Thompson enthusiasts, this tour is particularly interesting as it includes some of the craftsman's very last ecclesiastical work and examples of his fruitful collaboration with his friend, the architect JS Symes.

Harrogate

Fashionable boutiques, antique emporia, numerous cafés (including the famous Betty's Tea Room), hotels, museums and other tourist attractions are all contained within one of the loveliest towns in northern England. The town's popularity, which started to grow in the 1570s, really took off in 1848 with the coming of the railway. Visitors flocked to sample the supposed health-giving properties of the waters at numerous wells in and around the town. At the height of its popularity, it attracted royalty and aristocracy from all over Europe. In 1926, it was in the spotlight as the hiding place of crime writer Agatha Christie whose mysterious 'disappearance' attracted huge media coverage and public interest. The famous Pump Room in the centre of the town is now a museum and allows visitors a fascinating glimpse of the Spa in its heyday. At the Pump Room, visitors can also sample the waters, the sulphurous smell of which will appeal only to those of the strongest constitution. In the centre of the town, the famous Stray -

200 acres of open grassland and trees - provides excellent picnicking opportunities, as does the Valley Gardens with its delightful floral displays and pathways. For those who prefer to take their relaxation indoors, the town's famous Turkish Baths, in all their Victorian splendour, are a real treat.

Two churches close to the centre of the town contain fine examples of Thompson work. The first, Christ church, appears as a grey stone outcrop among the grassy acres of the Stray, to the south east of the town centre, close to the junction of York Place and Skipton Road.

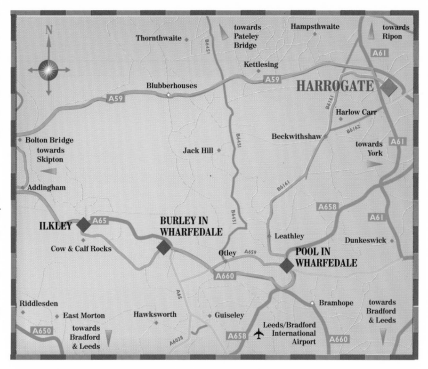

The church was constructed in 1831 at a cost of £4,500, much of it donated by wealthy benefactors, many of whom were visitors to Harrogate. The memorials inside the church and in the graveyard give a poignant insight into the large number of people who came to Harrogate from outside the region (and from abroad) presumably hoping for a cure and yet who ended their days in the town.

But there are also happier stories to be found inside the church, including one commemorated by Thompson – the altar rails, which are very early Thompson, were commissioned by the vicar, Canon Guy, in thanks for the safe return of his four sons from the Great War. The mouse can be found inside both the left and right rail.

To discover more church mice in Harrogate, head now for St Wilfrid's. Proceed back to the town centre to Parliament Street and out past the Turkish Baths on the road to Ripon. The fourth road on the left is Duchy Road. Turn down here and St Wilfrid's, a yellow stone church, is found a short distance on the left. The choir stalls are Thompson's along with a table in the north chapel. In the

Christ church, an oasis amidst Harrogate's famous Stray.

nave, three kneelers in front of the screen bear recessed mice and, in the Lady chapel, two kneelers are 'Mouseman' dated 1941.

It is now time to leave Harrogate and discover more of Thompson's work in Lower Wharfedale.

Leaving St Wilfrid's church, carry on along Duchy Road, turning right at the end of the road along Harlow Moor Road. Follow this road over a small stone bridge until it meets the B6161, Otley road, where our next destination, Pool, is sign-posted left eight miles. A short distance on, at Beckwithshaw village, you will pass signs to Harlow Carr Gardens, the home of the Northern Horticultural Society; it comprises 68 acres of landscaped and themed gardens as well as a coffee shop. Carry on through Beckwithshaw, over open countryside with delightful long-distance views, through Leathley village and on, then, to Pool-in-Wharfedale.

Pool-in-Wharfedale

This small village is centred on the convergence of several roads, linking Leeds, Skipton, Harrogate and Bradford. Apart from the fine views across the Wharfe to Leathley and Farnley - a base for artist JMW Turner during his tour of the north – there is little to detain the visitor here apart from the Methodist chapel where some of Robert Thompson's last work is found. The pieces within the chapel, including the pulpit, reredos, communion rails and table, were all completed in 1955, the year of Thompson's death. They also represent some of the final pieces in a long and fruitful artistic partnership between the Kilburn craftsman and a York architect, JS Syme. Further examples of this happy collaboration will be found at this tour's final destination, Ilkley. But, first, on to Burley-in-Wharfedale.

Burley-in-Wharfedale

Travelling to Burley-in-Wharfedale from Pool, one may choose to take either the top road (A660 towards Ilkley) which skirts the foot of the Chevin and offers fantastic long distance views along the Wharfe Valley or, alternatively, a lower road (A659) following the banks of the River Wharfe and through the centre of Otley. The former is more dramatic in terms of scenery whilst the latter offers a chance to sample the sights and sounds of the busy, unpretentious market town of Otley.

Both routes eventually merge on the far side of Otley and from here it is a straight run on a new road to Burley-in-Wharfedale. Approaching Burley, the blue clock face on the spire of St Mary the Virgin is clearly seen and this pinpoints the location of our next Thompson destination. Entering the village, the church is found on the right, opposite the village green.

Inside, Thompson's distinctive style makes the altar rails immediately recognisable as his work, which is just as well as the trademark mouse will not be found here should one seek it as a clue. There was a mouse once, but it is said that a lady parishioner, of nervous disposition but undoubtedly of great influence, objected to having to kneel next to it and it was duly removed! Other Robert Thompson pieces (all dating from the early 1950s) include the choir stalls, clergy stalls, pulpit and altar riddel posts. Later work, completed by the company after Robert Thompson's death, is represented by a lectern from the 1970s.

The Calf Rock, Ilkley Moor, looking across Wharfedale.

From Burley village to Ilkley, there is again a choice of a low road by the side of the River Wharfe, or a high road, skirting the moor. This time, the long-distance views from on high make the latter the better choice.

In the centre of Burley village, turn left at the mini roundabout, sign-posted to the station. The road leads up through Burley Woodhead towards the moor. At the top of the road, turn right and follow this road in the direction of Ilkley. You are now skirting the famous Ilkley Moor, part of the South Pennine Moors, designated as a site of special scientific interest. The moor is renowned for its bird life including curlew, golden plover, peregrine and merlin – all are shy birds and visitors are more likely to see wood pigeons and grouse, which are plentiful on the moor.

The road rises steeply, offering superb long-distance views along the Wharfe Valley. On a clear day you can see for miles; when it is misty, the eerie qualities of the wilderness are heightened; on a winter's day, the snow-covered moor is breathtaking. In fact, whatever, the weather, this drive will enchant even the most weary traveller. The real drama of the tour is reached at the famous Cow and Calf Rocks. These mighty boulders perch precariously on the edge of the moor and offer a dramatic practice ground for rock climbers. Turning the corner by the rocks, the view opens up into a quite breathtaking panorama with Ilkley town spread out below and views way up the dale beyond. The road now drops sharply into the town centre.

Ilkley

Ilkley is almost always immediately associated with the Yorkshire anthem 'On Ilkla Moor baht 'at'. A walk on the moor is recommended for anyone interested in natural history, geology, Bronze Age stone carvings or, of course, simply to blow the cobwebs away. Ilkley also has much to offer down in the town. In Roman times, the town - known as Olicana - was a strategic base and crossing point of the Wharfe. The town's museum, which is housed in the old manor house, is built on the site of the Roman fort and

Robert Thompson (left) with his life-long friend, the architect JS Syme, at Ilkley parish church in 1953. This was one of their last joint ventures together.

Gravestones outside Ilkley parish church.

contains interesting Roman artifacts and reconstructions of the fort. The museum also provides a potted history of the town after the departure of the Romans, including its Victorian heyday as a spa town built around the supposed curative powers of the moorland spring up at White Wells. Today, many of the town's former hydropathic institutes are hotels or retirement homes. The sight of these imposing, ivy-clad buildings allows one's mind to wander back to a time when 'water cures' and a restorative stay in Ilkley were the height of fashion among polite society.

Just next to the Manor House museum is the parish church of All Saints, also built on the site of the Roman fort of Olicana. The present building is partly mediaeval but was largely re-built in Victorian times. Inside, Thompson enthusiasts and organ lovers alike will be fascinated with the organ cases, which were a collaborative effort between Robert Thompson and the architect and designer, JS Syme of York. The cases won the Organ Club's prize for the best new organ cases when they were completed in 1953 - they were also one of the last major commissions carried out by

Robert Thompson himself. It is interesting to note that the mouse on each of these pieces is recessed rather than carved in relief. This was to deter souvenir hunters who at that time were 'bagging' Thompson mice, much to the annoyance of Robert Thompson and the owners of the furniture.

There are many other points of interest in the church including the 13th century doorway with distinctive dogtooth moulding. Earlier still are the exquisitely carved Saxon crosses, the presence of which indicate that Ilkley must have been an important ecclesiastical centre in Anglo-Saxon times. Oak boxed pews and the font from the 17th century are also of interest as is the effigy of Sir Adam Middelton, a member of the dominant Middelton clan whose ancient family seat can be seen overlooking the town.

From the parish church, head up Brook Street, the town's main thoroughfare. At the top of the street, take Wells Road, which rises steeply towards Ilkley Moor.

49

Visitors with time to spare may wish to carry on to the top of Wells Road and then walk up to White Wells, the ancient bathhouse into which an ice-cold moorland spring emerges. Once teams of donkeys carried invalids and visitors to this primitive plunge-pool, which was recommended as a cure for all types of ailments. Today, the hardy (or foolhardy) may immerse themselves in the chilly waters on New Year's Day. The building is open most days – look to see if the flag is flying over the building. From White Wells, the views are magnificent: across to Barden Moor up the Wharfe Valley or back towards Otley and Leeds, they make it well worth the steep walk and highlight Ilkley's position as the gateway to the Dales.

Halfway up Wells Road, look out for three stone steps which mark the site of an old donkey station. Turn right here onto Queens Road and St Margaret's church is a couple of hundred yards along on the left. Here are found Thompson's mice on the altar rails, candlesticks, chairs in the Lady Chapel and on a memorial board to previous vicars. Across the road from the church is a large enclosed stone, upon which may be seen bronze age carvings similar to those found on Ilkley Moor.

Leaving Ilkley, the route continues on the A65 in the direction of Skipton, through Addingham, on towards Bolton Bridge and over Blubberhouses Moor. At the top of the moor, the unsuspecting visitor receives a jolt with the surreal juxtaposition of space age technology and natural wilderness at the US Airbase at Menwith Hill. In fact, no matter how many times one passes the site, the huge white 'golf balls' never fail to fascinate. After Menwith, it is just a short drive into Harrogate and the end of a varied and stimulating day's tour.

Geoff Lund

51

A view of Ilkley from White Wells.

Chapter nine

The Upper Dales
(70 Miles)

This tour is crammed full of history and also takes in some of the most scenic areas of Wharfedale, Nidderdale and Swaledale. En route, visitors will discover Thompson's work brushing shoulders with Saxon remains at Ripon Cathedral and military artifacts at the Green Howards museum in Richmond.

It also allows visitors to pay homage to two Yorkshire 'greats': William Bromflet, the mediaeval woodcarver whose work in Ripon Cathedral so inspired the young Robert Thompson; and the much-loved Yorkshire writer, JB Priestley, whose final resting place is to be found in the quiet graveyard at Hubberholme. Other historical 'personalities' encountered on this tour include Lewis Carroll and Mary Queen of Scots.

Ripon

The cathedral church of St Peter and St Wilfrid dominates the picturesque huddle of ancient buildings and winding streets that make up Ripon, one of the smallest cathedral cities in England. The cathedral's Saxon crypt was founded by St Wilfrid in 672 AD, whilst the main building was built between 1154 and 1530.

Before seeking Thompson's work in the cathedral, visitors should first seek out the misericords in the choir carved by William Bromflet and his school, between 1489 and 1494. Bromflet's carvings were an inspiration for Thompson and help to place his work in context.

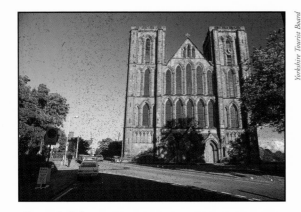

Yorkshire Tourist Board

Ripon cathedral.

A carved bench end from Ripon cathedral. The picture is from a large collection of photographs of mediaeval carvings which Thompson used as reference in his own work.

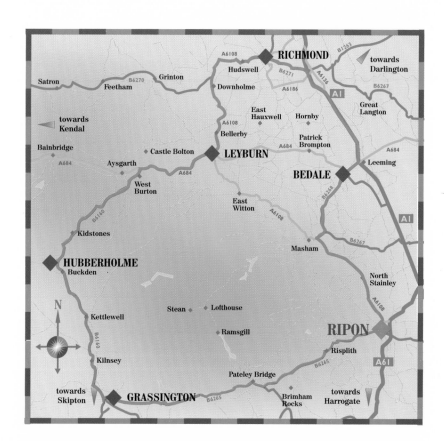

The Ripon misericords present finely carved depictions of well-known biblical scenes, merged with secular images - such as hunting scenes - and pagan or mythical figures, which combine to provide a fascinating insight into the life and psyche of mediaeval folk. Detailed descriptions and explanations of all the misericord carvings are provided by the cathedral. Look out particularly on the north side for the dancing pigs, playing bagpipes; St Cuthman wheeling his aged mother in a wheel barrow; and the 'pelican' shedding its own blood to feed its children - perhaps never having seen a pelican, the carver's image is closer to that of a swan! On the south side, a carving of a fox preaching to a goose is a satirical depiction of travelling friars and other unscrupulous clerics. At the end of this row is a picture of a rabbit caught by a griffin, whilst in the background another rabbit disappears down its burrow. This image is famed as Lewis Carroll's inspiration for Alice in Wonderland - his father was Canon of Ripon from 1852 to 1868.

Some of the mediaeval misericords from Ripon cathedral that inspired the young Robert Thompson.

information station near the north door. Also, at the north door reception is a fine chair with a curved back and webbed leather seat. It bears the head of a ram and another beast at the end of each arm. A partner chair also exists in the Chapter House.

In addition to the work of Bromflet and Thompson, there is much to admire in the cathedral. Visitors with limited time will be rewarded by a visit to the Treasury (a small entrance fee is payable) which contains the Saxon 'Ripon Jewel'. This small but exquisite roundel was found in 1976 close to the cathedral. It is dated to the time of St Wilfrid (c670 AD) and was probably made as a decoration for a relic casket or cross.

Also of interest and dating from the earliest period of the cathedral's history is the crypt. The vaulted stone ceiling in the main chamber is unique in England.

Leaving the cathedral, visitors may wish to explore the streets, shops and museums of Ripon before returning to the car to continue the tour.

We shall meet up again with Lewis Carroll (and fantasy animals) later in the tour in Richmond.

Having examined Bromflet's work, visitors will be eager to compare it with Thompson's. The Kilburn craftsman's early work is demonstrated in St Wilfrid's chapel (close to the north door) by a pair of tall candlesticks with blue coloured decoration. Produced in the 1920s, these are without the mouse trademark and yet are immediately identifiable by the rugged, adzed finish. A further set of slightly smaller candlesticks, dated 1937, 1942 and c.1945 are now used for funeral services. Stored in the Chapter House, they are not readily available for public viewing.

As Thompson gave new life to the style and technique of Bromflet, so too the 'Mouseman's' tradition was continued in the cathedral by his successors. In the library, at the top of the wooden stairs, is a long, low cupboard with four panelled doors. The mouse is clearly seen at the front on the left leg. A memorial plaque confirms its date of 1969 and its partner, a desk, is located at the

From Ripon, take the B6265 road to Pateley Bridge. One quickly comes upon the walls of Studley Royal Park and Fountains Abbey. Here are found the most complete remains of a Cistercian abbey in Britain as well as spectacular 18th century landscaped gardens and a deer park. There is a full and diverse programme of activities in the Park all year round, phone ahead for details.

Continuing on into Nidderdale, the road leads over moorland and past signs to Brimham Rocks. The rocks, which are situated just over a mile from the main road, have been weathered into dramatic shapes, presenting a weird, slightly sinister atmosphere.

The main road starts to drop down into the busy, riverside town of Pateley Bridge which offers a wide range of simple, countryside tourist attractions. A steep climb on the B6265 road, from Nidderdale to Wharfedale, goes over Greenhow to Grassington, a suitable 'half-way house' between Ripon and our next 'Mouseman' location, Hubberholme.

Grassington

This delightful Dales village is a mecca for tourists and can be quite crowded in the summer. Nonetheless, its narrow cobbled streets and market square retain a simple 'olde worlde' charm. Park in the main car park, which is also the site for the National Park information centre and is just a few hundred yards from the village centre. In the village are all the usual amenities plus interesting craft and antique shops that one expects in a tourist honey-pot.

For history lovers, Grassington offers a great deal and first stop must be the folk museum situated right in the market square. From the village centre, there are also a number of walks of historic interest including up on to Grassington Moor where relics of the village's lead mining heritage may be found. Other footpaths lead to the sites of Bronze Age and Iron Age settlements and include the finest example of a Celtic field system in the Dales.

From the car park, in the opposite direction to the village centre, it is just a short walk down to the river where the tumbling waters of Linton Falls are

Linton Falls near Grassington.

crossed by the 'Tin Bridge'. A pretty walk past the redundant Linton Mill, by the riverside cottages and along to Linton church provides an opportunity for drivers to stretch their legs and enjoy the bird song and natural beauty of this secluded beauty spot. Then it is back to the car park and off again to Hubberholme,

Hubberholme

From Grassington, the trail (B6160) leads up the Wharfe Valley to Buckden and onto Hubberholme. The church of St Michael and All Angels sits on the banks of the Wharfe and is distinguished for having one of the few rood lofts left in Yorkshire. It is also famed as the final resting place of the great Yorkshire author, JB Priestley, whose ashes are buried here. Inside, Thompson's skills are demonstrated in the pews and choir stalls, completed in 1933 and 34.

Having recrossed the river to the church, continue on the unclassified road and rejoin the B6160 at Cray. Turn left and

accompany the gurgling beck down Bishopdale to the picturesque village of West Burton. On meeting the A684, turn right for the market town of Leyburn. A detour can be made at this point to Aysgarth Falls to see the foaming waters of the River Ure and Bolton Castle where Mary Queen of Scots was imprisoned.

Leyburn

Leyburn has a no-nonsense, down-to-earth appearance and is no less attractive for it. Comprising mainly Georgian and Victorian stone buildings around the market square, the town is steeped in history. The main street is expansive to accommodate its Friday market - an institution here since it moved to the town in the 1680s when the dominant market town of Wensley was decimated by the plague.

The parish church of St Matthew is passed on the right as one enters the town. Due to its location on this main road, it is perhaps easier to drive on a short distance and park in the Market Place and then walk back to the church.

Fountains Abbey.

Hubberholme church.

The church was built in 1868. Inside, Thompson's work is revealed in the form of the lectern, pulpit and prie-dieu, dating from 1940 to 1946.

From Leyburn, follow the A6108 towards Richmond, heading over the moors via Bellerby and past the firing ranges of Catterick Camp. Passing through Downholme, the route follows the course of the River Swale through a dramatic steep-sided, craggy faced and heavily wooded valley, leading to Richmond.

Richmond

Richmond, the ancient market town of Swaledale, is dominated by the brooding presence of its Norman castle. Open to the public, the castle's parapets, and the promenade round the castle exterior provide fantastic

Yorkshire Tourist Board

The view from Richmond Tower, looking down onto the market square and the Green Howards' regimental museum.

long-distance views. In the town, the winding streets offer something of interest at every turn, including a beautifully preserved Georgian theatre. The history of Richmond is intertwined with that of the Green Howards, one of Britain's oldest and most famous army regiments. Thompson's work is located within the regimental chapel (in the church of St Mary the Virgin) and in the regimental museum, which is located in the town's market square.

Head first for the church, which is located on the outskirts of the town centre about five minutes' walk from the market place. The exact date of the church's foundation is unknown but it certainly dates back before 1147. However, it was subject to extensive modernisation work in 1857. Before entering the church, it is interesting to explore the churchyard which includes a number of fascinating graves including, on the north side of the church, the plague stone which marks the site of a communal grave. The churchyard also offers us another link to Charles Lutwidge Dodgson (better known as Lewis Carroll) who played here whilst a pupil at Richmond School from 1844. Inside the church, the misericords under the seats in the choir are worthy of note. These seats were brought to the church from nearby Easby Abbey following the dissolution of the monasteries. Some of the carvings - the bagpipe-playing pigs and other fantastical creatures - remind us of Bromflet's carvings in Ripon. It is tempting to think that these images sowed seeds in the young Lewis Carroll's fervent imagination.

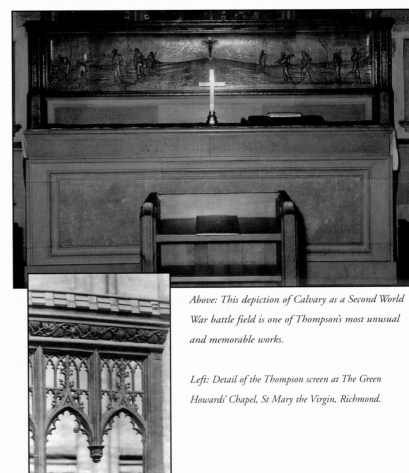

Above: This depiction of Calvary as a Second World War battle field is one of Thompson's most unusual and memorable works.

Left: Detail of the Thompson screen at The Green Howards' Chapel, St Mary the Virgin, Richmond.

In the church, Thompson's work completed between 1933 and 1945 dominates the Green Howards' chapel, which commemorates members of the regiment who died in the two world wars. Thompson's mice are found here on the screen (on the left hand post at the entrance to the chapel), on the chairs, altar rails, two altar stools (inscribed Scarborough and Beverley), a prie-dieu and chair. But the jewel in this particular treasury of Thompson work is the outstanding reredos. This bas-relief presents a 20th century interpretation of Calvary. Christ on the crucifix is transposed to a battle field scene from the Second World War. Eight soldiers and two grave diggers prepare graves for the fallen against a background of blasted, bomb-damaged buildings. The piece is heart rending both in its juxtaposition of images and the skill and artistry of its execution.

From the church, it is just a short walk back to the market place and the Green Howards' regimental museum. Set in a converted 12th century church, the museum's collection spans the 300-year history of this famous regiment. The Thompson furniture here was originally produced for the officers' and sergeants' messes in the regiment's depot.

Leaving Richmond, drive back towards St Mary the Virgin church and follow the signs for the A1 south towards Bedale. The route takes you in the direction of Easby Abbey. In fact, there is a pleasant riverside walk from Richmond Castle to Easby Abbey (a distance of about five miles). Visitors hoping to complete this full 'mouse tour' in one day are unlikely to have time to fit in this walk but it can be earmarked for a separate day. On the A1 travel south turning off on the A684 to Bedale.

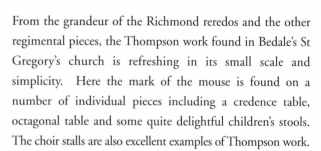

Bedale

Bedale is one of Yorkshire's smallest market towns. The church of St Gregory at its centre dates back to an earlier Saxon church, which was given a north aisle towards the end of the 12th century and a south aisle a century later. The imposing tower is said to have been built as a refuge from border raiders.

From the grandeur of the Richmond reredos and the other regimental pieces, the Thompson work found in Bedale's St Gregory's church is refreshing in its small scale and simplicity. Here the mark of the mouse is found on a number of individual pieces including a credence table, octagonal table and some quite delightful children's stools. The choir stalls are also excellent examples of Thompson work.

Before leaving the church, take time to view the monuments. An alabaster knight, Sir Brian Fitzalan, Lord Lieutenant of Scotland, is shown with chain mail garb and flowing curls, his wife by his side. Dating from the early 14th century, this is considered to be one of the finest examples of mediaeval sculpture in the country.

It is now just a short drive back to Ripon (on the B6268 and A6108), arriving in time to hear the horn blower at 9pm herald the close of the day.

Chapter ten

The Lake District

(70 Miles)

This 70-mile round trip offers a busy one-day dash or a more leisurely weekend tour, through delightful countryside, with plenty of fine Mouseman pieces as highlights en route and many opportunities to take in the beauty spots of Lakeland.

Ambleside

The popular town of Ambleside at the north end of Lake Windermere makes an excellent starting point for this scenic tour. Our first destination is Ambleside's parish church but on the way into town from the main car park, it is worth pausing for a quick look at a curious little building called Bridge House. Perched over Stock Ghyll, this tiny one-up, one-down former summer house was the home of a less

View from Kirkstone Pass descending to Patterdale.

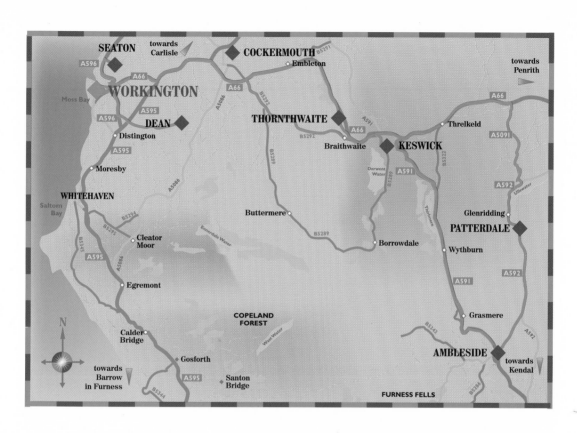

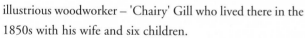

illustrious woodworker – 'Chairy' Gill who lived there in the 1850s with his wife and six children.

At around the same time as the Gills were crammed into Bridge House, the Victorian architect, Sir George Gilbert Scott, was busy with the construction of Ambleside's gothic parish church of St. Mary the Virgin (completed in 1854). To reach it cross Stock Low Bridge and leave the bustle of the town centre behind, turning down Compston Road and then into Vicarage Road (by the cinema). Inside St Mary's

Wordsworth Chapel is a modern 'mouse' piece: a panel on the east wall, commissioned in the 1980s by the church's curate, in memory of her mother.

Back in the car, head northeast out of Ambleside on an unclassified road signposted for Kirkstone. This road is also known as 'The Struggle' but is well worth the effort for its excellent views. Having met up with the A592, continue north through the Kirkstone pass - near the top there is an opportunity to pause and admire the views, as well as the delights of the Kirkstone Pass Inn (England's third highest pub). Carry on down the other side, past Brotherswater to Patterdale, our next Mouseman spot.

Patterdale

Surrounded by steep fells, the mid-19th century church of St Patrick is between Patterdale and Glenridding on the shores of Ullswater. On display in the church is a pair of staves with Thompson's distinctive fine-adzed finish. The staves are decorated in colour – one with the shamrock of St Patrick and the other with a Bishop's mitre. On the reverse of each is a shield with the legend 'E.A.H. 1955' and a mouse carved in bas relief. Both mice are complete with paws; on the Shamrock stave, the tail is curved under its body, whilst on the Mitre stave it dangles down over the shield.

Yorkshire Tourist Board

St Patrick's church is between Patterdale and Glenridding on the shores of Ullswater.

Other features to look out for at the church are tapestry panels by Ann Macbeth (1875-1948) - a leading embroidress, who lived in Patterdale. One of them - 'The Nativity' - is loaned to the church each summer by the Glasgow Corporation. Another -'The Good Shepherd' - depicts Christ as a shepherd, against a backdrop of Lakeland fells, including Hartsop, Deepdale, Caudale Moor and Kirkstone. The music to the hymn 'Jerusalem' is at the bottom of the tapestry and the story goes that Queen Mary liked it so much, she burst into song when she saw it for the first time!

From Patterdale, carry on alongside Ullswater to the A5091, which will take you towards Keswick, through Dockray and Matterdale End. Before leaving Ullswater, it is worth making a quick detour on foot to the magnificent Aira Force waterfall, which offers a dramatic picnic spot and pleasant woodland stroll (National Trust car parks are by the lake and a short way up the Dockray road).

Take the A66 towards Keswick, where the shops and attractions of this busy market town offer a tempting place to stop off - especially if you have opted to spread this tour over more than one day.

Thornthwaite

The next destination is the church of St Mary, in the village of Thornthwaite. The village is located on a loop of unclassified road just off the A66 between Keswick and Bassenthwaite Lake. St Mary's church was originally built in the mid-1700s but then later remodelled in the early 19th century. Inside, mouse-seekers will immediately home in on the Bishop's chair, usually located beside the altar. Carved by Thompson, it is decorated with a coat of arms picked out in blue and the mouse is to be found scurrying along its top edge.

If you are keen on local arts and crafts, Thornthwaite Gallery is well worth a visit before leaving the village - it displays and sells works by local artists and during the summer months there are often craft demonstrations too.

The Mouseman tour provides opportunity to combine 'art' with 'craft' by taking in some important sights linked to Britain's most famous poet, William Wordworth.

Return by car back to the A66 and head west towards Seaton. Fans of Wordsworth may not be able to resist a brief detour to Cockermouth, to visit the birthplace of the ultimate romantic and Wordsworth House - the poet's childhood home. This has been restored by the National Trust and the house and gardens are opened at selected times from April to November.

Back on the Mouseman trail, carry on towards Workington. Two miles to the northeast is Seaton and the church of St Paul – our next destination.

Seaton

This small village church was built in 1883 by George Watson of Keswick and is a chapel of ease to the nearby church of St Peter, Camerton. The work here is more recent and includes choir stalls, two prie-dieux and the pulpit. All the pieces were commissioned by the mother of John Fisher, who was Church Warden at St Paul's from 1951-1970; the book ledge on the south choir stalls carries a carved inscription in his memory.

Beautiful Keswick is the half-way point on this tour. Shown here is the view from Keswick landing stage across to Derwent Isle with Castlerigg Fell in the distance.

Workington

On now, to one of the highlights of the tour - the collection of Thompson carved pieces at the town's Benedictine priory of Our Lady, Star of the Sea and St. Michael. To find the priory, go northwest up Workington High Street, which then becomes Guard Street. Turn left into Bank Street and continue into Banklands, where you will find the priory. It was built in 1876, with typically geometrical Victorian features on the outside but inside is a treasure trove of vintage and more modern Mouseman carving.

The early pieces include the choir stalls - pre-mouse - complete with a fascinating set of misericords that show scenes from Aesop's Fables. One of the bench ends has a scene depicting a donkey in a pulpit, a symbolic warning against listening to preaching fools and false teachers. Look out on the north (altar) side of the choir for a multi-purpose stand, which is just the job for stowing away awkward ecclesiastical accessories, such as banners, processional crosses or candle snuffers.

The more recent 'mouse-work' has the characteristic raised mouse of the

second generation of carvers and includes a lectern and three leaflet/magazine tables with nicely carved ends.

Before heading back inland, Workington Hall offers a quick historical detour - the house, originally built in 1379, was visited by Mary Queen of Scots, after she fled Scotland in 1568.

Dean

The last port of call is another feast of Thompson carving – the church of St Oswald in Dean.

Dean is about 10 miles to the south east, on the way from Workington to

View over Ashness Bridge and the Vale of Keswick.

Loweswater. The church is a venerable, 800-year-old place of worship that was given a Kilburn makeover in the late 1960s. There are apparently 20 'mice' inside the church and it is quite a challenge to locate them all. From August 1967 through to April 1968, the Thompson carvers completely refurnished the chancel, designing its new layout and supplying choir stalls, the pulpit, two priest's stalls, a lectern, all the pews and the front panel.

Also look out for the gargoyles - a rare breed in this part of the world - St Oswald's is one of only three churches in Cumbria to contain them. Also of interest is an ancient preaching cross in the

Choir stalls at Workington hark back to Bromflet's work at Ripon, particularly in their depiction of mythological beasts.

An unusual stand at Workington Priory produced in 1922. Robert Thompson took this photograph prior to the piece's installation. His caption states that it represents the 'four ages of man, or the four seasons of the year.'

Right: A kneeler for Workington Priory. Thompson's own description of the carvings was that it showed 'the devil chained and a suspicious character handcuffed.'

graveyard, which dates back to the 12th century or earlier and is believed to have been used by the monks at Calder Abbey.

To round off this Lakeland mouse-odyssey, make your way back across to Keswick - you can choose between the forested slopes of the Whinlatter Pass (B5292) or the dramatic screes and quarries of the winding Honister Pass (B5289). After a restorative tour of the tearooms, head south to Grasmere for Wordsworth's home, Dove Cottage, and his final resting place in St Oswald's churchyard, before arriving back at your start point in Ambleside.

Chapter eleven

York
the Mouse City

The ancient city of York offers such an array of history, architecture, pageant and other diversions that there is far too much to absorb in one day.

Following the trail of the mouse gives a special focus to a visit to the city: for first-timers as well as those who have been many times and have trod the traditional tourist routes. During this visit, you will take in the city's crown jewel - the Minster - and also some hidden gems that the 'hurry-scurry' of many York tourist trails pass by.

If arriving by car, park in the car park off Marygate just west of Bootham Bar. Leaving the car park, you will emerge onto Marygate. Proceed left towards Bootham.

Passengers arriving by train, from the station, head towards the city over Lendal Bridge. Once you have crossed the bridge, take the steps down to the river bank and follow the river west, with the gardens on your right. At Marygate, turn right, passing the car park on your left.

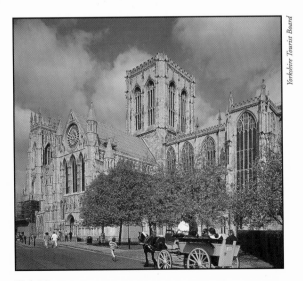

Yorkshire Tourist Board

York Minster.

St Olave's

Half way along Marygate on your right is St Olave's church. The dim light makes mouse spotting here particularly difficult. However, the pews in the chapel on the south side of the chancel are unmistakably Thompson. Chunky and heavily adzed with unusual castellated moulding, they date from c1936. The mouse is found on the front of the kneelers.

From St Olave's, continue along Marygate by the side of the Abbey walls, which date from the 13th and 14th centuries. At Bootham, turn right, on through Bootham Bar, passing the art gallery on your right and proceed up to the Minster.

The Minster

York Minster presents an awe-inspiring setting for some of Thompson's finest work. During the period 1935 to 1956, the Dean and Chapter of the Minster commissioned a large body of internal decorative work from two distinguished architects, Sir Charles Peers and his successor, Sir Albert Edward Richardson, President of the Royal Academy.

The execution of these designs was entrusted to Robert Thompson, demonstrating how the Kilburn wood carver's reputation had reached the highest levels of architectural and ecclesiastical sensibilities.

The KOYLI Chapel

Entering the Minster through the main west doorway, you head for the chapel dedicated to The King's Own Light Infantry (or KOYLIs as they are

popularly known). Here, a glass-fronted bookcase (from 1947) and a roll of honour of soldiers killed in action are unmistakably Robert Thompson's work.

Bishop Savage's Chantry

Moving on a short way down this aisle, the next Thompson creation is a hidden gem and something of a surprise. On the right, above the 16th century tomb of Bishop Savage is a chantry designed by the architect Albert Richardson. Completed by Robert Thompson in 1950, this small chapel on high is designed to accommodate two people and is accessed from the high altar. Ornately carved wood with detail highlighted in gold and embroidered cloth at the sides, the Dean and Chapter of the cathedral praised Thompson 'for his brilliant execution of a design so different in character and detail from his customary work, it will stand as witness to posterity of our own generation's creative and executive ability, for we can show so few works of the standard of the past ages'.

Above: Work destined for York Minster, photographed in Robert Thompson's workshop prior to installation.

Inset top: Bishop Savage's Chantry

Inset right: The Archbishop's Chair on the high altar, dedicated to Bishop Woollcombe.

St Stephen's Chapel

On to St Stephen's Chapel at the east end of the north choir aisle where Thompson's mouse identifies the stall as his work. Completed in 1946, these pieces were the first he realised for architect Albert Richardson.

Lady Chapel

Next to St Stephen's is the Lady Chapel. Eight oak seats are fitted into the stone screen behind which is the high altar. The prie-dieux are carved with delicate foliage and the mouse lurks on the side panels of the two outer prie-dieux and the central one. Thompson carried out this work in 1945 with lecterns for the chapel supplied the following year.

High Altar and Sanctuary

Turning now to the other side of the stone screen is the high altar and sanctuary. The Archbishop's chair here is a superb Thompson piece. On the north side of the sanctuary are five Deans' stalls with lace curtain effect tracery carved from the oak of the prie-dieux. Opposite these are three chairs and prie-dieux and servers' stalls. Whilst the rippled oak surfaces

York Minster, seen from the city walls near Lendal Bridge.

immediately identify these as 'Thompson', the enthusiast may be puzzled by the lack of the trademark mouse. In fact, Thompson was simply following strict instructions from the Dean who insisted that the altar should not be over-run with mice: no more than one mouse to every three stalls!

The Consistory Court

Before leaving the Minster, visitors should, if possible, seek access to the Consistory Court - special permission may be required. Here Thompson's work - the judge's seat and cupboard - is quite magnificent: the strong yet controlled carving and adzed ripples complement the sense of authority and tradition that is exuded by this small, enclosed court room.

To exit the Minster, leave by the south door. Immediately outside and to the right of the door take a look at the notice board. There is no mouse here and yet, although weather-beaten, the quality of the carving and the adzed finish are unmistakably Thompson's.

St William's College

Turning left now outside the south door and following the green round

69

the east end of the Minster leads into College Street. Founded in 1461, the college building offers a quiet courtyard behind heavy double doors studded with iron. It is these doors that attract our attention for a close examination of the right door shows the tell-tale mouse nestling within one of the upper panels. His partner on the left door has long since disappeared.

Having explored St William's College (and perhaps enjoyed refreshments here) retrace your steps back to the south door of the Minster. Take the path opposite which is signposted to The Shambles, then turn left down Low Petergate. Note at this junction, on the corner of High Petergate, a figure of Minerva, goddess of wisdom. Carry on past Grape Lane and into King's Square. Cross the square, turning right into King's Court and then left into The Shambles.

The Shambles is one of the oldest streets in York. The name comes from 'shamel', meaning stalls or benches on which meat is displayed, a reference to the old butchers' quarter of the city. Today, the narrow street of The

All Saints church - carved screen with symbols representing Christ's Passion and Crucifixion.

Shambles is invariably bustling with tourists and shoppers. Half way along the street, look out for the house of Margaret Clitheroe on the right. One of York's catholic martyrs, she met her death in 1586. Today, her house is preserved as a simple shrine; largely overlooked by the tourist throng, it provides a welcome haven for quiet contemplation.

All Saints, Pavement

At the end of The Shambles, you emerge onto Pavement and turn right here. This was one of the first mediaeval streets to have a paved way.

It was formerly the scene of public gatherings, including executions. All Saints church now lies straight ahead. In years gone by, a fire was lit every night in the lantern tower to guide travellers to York through the Forest of Galtres.

Two massive organ cases dominate with the mouse recessed on the right case. The work was carried out by Robert Thompson's successors in the early 1960s but the master's inspiration is clearly evident.

In addition, two prieu-dieux are sited in front of the altar, again with a recessed mouse on the right. The panels on the left and right of the reredos are finely crafted with symbols representing the Passion and Crucifixion of Christ.

Leaving the church, turn onto Parliament Street, a wide, paved thoroughfare which is usually home to various street performers. Carry on into Davygate, past Betty's famous tea rooms, look out for their own brand 'mouse bread' displayed in wooden bowls carved by the craftsmen in Kilburn. Proceed across St Helen's Square into Lendal and then left at Museum Street.

Above and top: pieces destined for St Clement's, York. Photographed by Robert Thompson in his workshop.

Follow the road down to the River Ouse. Carry on straight over Lendal Bridge to return to the train station.

To return to the car park, do not cross over Lendal Bridge, instead take the steps down to the river bank and then follow the path alongside the gardens on the right. This pleasant riverside walk eventually leads to Marygate. Turn right here and the car park is then on your left.

At this point, you may wish to conclude the tour but if time (and weary legs) allow, visits to St Chad's and St Clement's are highly recommended as they are home to some really beautiful pieces of Thompson work.

St Chad's

As this church is situated someway off the beaten track (approximately one mile outside the city centre) it is recommended to check in advance that access is available so that your visit is not in vain. From the city centre, head in the direction of the station and then follow Queen Street out to Micklegate Bar. This was traditionally the monarch's entrance into the city and was also the site upon which traitors' heads were displayed. From here, follow signs to the racecourse along Blossom Street and then The Mount. Just before the racecourse, turn left into Knavesmire Road. St Chad's, an unprepossessing red brick building, is situated a short distance along on the left.

It is well worth the trip as, inside, the pulpit is Thompson's work as are two leather-seated chairs for the Bishop and Officiant, the font cover and two oak alms dishes.

St Clement's

To reach St Clement's, carry on past St Chad's until you meet Bishopthorpe Road, turn left and then second left into Scarcroft Road. The church is on your right.

The pieces here are early Thompson and are on a par with those found at Workington Priory. St Clement's is considered to be home to some of Thompson's finest work.

Chapter twelve

Further afield

Robert Thompson outside his workshop in Kilburn with the credence table destined for Westminster Abbey.

Robert Thompson lived, worked and died in Kilburn but his work travelled far. The index at the end of this book provides a list of Thompson's commissions across the country. Some particular highlights are noted below, along with contemporary pieces which bring the story right up to date.

Westminster Abbey

Robert Thompson received a commission in 1942 to provide two large standing altar candlesticks as a memorial to men who perished when HMS Barham was sunk in the Mediterranean the previous year. The candlesticks are unusual examples of Thompson work as the detail is picked out in blue, red and gold. Although there are other examples of coloured candlesticks, including some at Ripon cathedral, Thompson did not favour the use of colour believing that the natural hue of the wood should be enough to carry the design of a piece.

The candlesticks were installed and dedicated at a memorial service in February 1943 and are decorated every year with a floral tribute at a memorial service organised by the survivors of HMS Barham. Following their installation, a second commission followed from the widow of the Barham's Commanding Officer, Captain GC Cook, for a pair of two-foot candlesticks for the nave altar. Having received the commission on 7th October 1943, Robert Thompson made extra effort to deliver the work quickly. A postcard response confirms this, he wrote: "I will do my best to have the Altar candlesticks completed for the date you mention, but really cannot promise to do so as I have a great deal of work in hand, and labour is very difficult these days. However, you know I will do my best." And so he did, the candlesticks were delivered in less than seven weeks, in time for the memorial service on 25th November 1943.

Also in the Abbey is a credence table. Dating from the same time as the candlesticks, it commemorates the wife of the Bishop of Chichester.

Commissions for Westminster Abbey are an accolade and demonstrate just how far Thompson's reputation had spread among leading architects and the great and the good.

Brecon Cathedral

The work in Brecon Cathedral was completed after Robert Thompson's death - it was dedicated by the Bishop of Swansea and Brecon in 1963. However, it clearly demonstrates the continuance of his ideas and the inspiration he found in the work of mediaeval craftsmen. The magnificent oak screen in the Cordwainers chapel was commissioned by the London architect ADR Caroe (a firm with which Robert Thompson had forged a

strong working relationship). The piece was commissioned as a continuation of a mediaeval screen, which runs along one side of the chapel.

The Kilburn screen comprises two panels, one of which depicts a goat's head, the Cordwainers' traditional emblem. The other panel shows the tools of the shoemakers' and leather workers' trades. The screen is topped with fine tracery with the 'mouse' appearing at the foot of the far right column.

The screen at Brecon Cathedral, a continuation of the mediaeval tradition which inspired Thompson.

Bangor Cathedral

The work in Bangor Cathedral started in 1954, just before Robert Thompson's death the following year, and was completed in 1960.

The earliest piece is the screen at the east end of the north aisle in the north transept. A second screen followed in 1960 at the east end of the south aisle in the north transept. A fine font cover is also from the Kilburn workshop.

Following his commissions from Ampleforth, appreciation of Thompson's work spread within the Catholic community. Two locations with fine examples of his work are noted below.

Pluscarden Priory

The Benedictine priory at Pluscarden near Elgin in Moray dates from 1230. Superb examples of Thompson's work are the misericords on the choir stalls in the chancel in the Abbey Church. Whilst the Abbey Church is open 365 days a year, visits to the chancel are only by prior arrangement, upon which, one of the monks will be happy to show Thompson's work. To make arrangements, telephone 01343 890257.

73

Canna, Isle of Hebrides

The Roman Catholic church of St Edward was built by a former Marquis of Bute. Inside the church, the oak communion rail, complete with 'mouse' was originally donated to Glenforsa Chapel by the Beale family of Glenforsa. When the chapel closed, it was taken to Canna, arriving there circa 1953.

Elmore Abbey

Work at Elmore Abbey was completed in 1995 comprising seven choir stalls, nave benches and sacristy furniture.

Suggested design for stalls in English oak for Elmore Abbey, Speen, Newbury.

The Green Dragon Inn, Cockleford Nr Cheltenham, Gloucestershire.

The bar was refurbished by Robert Thompson's Craftsmen Limited in the mid 1990s.

And even further ...

Thompson's legacy continues today through the craftsmen at Kilburn, whose work reaches the furthest corners of the earth. From Kilburn to Katmandu, the mouse has travelled far.

Speaker's Chair for the Nepalese Parliment.

INDEX OF ROBERT THOMPSON'S WORK

Compiled by Christopher Scaife, Kilburn

The following index is currently the most comprehensive guide to all work completed by Robert Thompson up to approximately 1948. Details are taken from the workbooks kept by Robert Thompson which are now in the archives at the family firm, Robert Thompson's Craftsmen Limited, in Kilburn.

Belmont	Durham	St Mary Magdelene	Pews, table	
Benfield Side	Durham	Parish church	Credence table	1938
Berkeley	Somerset	St Mary the Virgin	Stalls	1948-59
Berkswell	Warcs.	Rectory	Altar rails, candlesticks, altar, reredos,	1929-48
Berkswell	Warcs.	St John the Baptist	Pulpit, font, altar rail	1927-30
Beverley	Yorks.E	Minster	Memorial chapel	1947
Beverley	Yorks.E	St Mary	Kneelers	1945
Beverley	Yorks.E	St Mary	Memorial door, panels	1956
Bexhill on Sea	Sussex.E	St Barnabas	Bishop's chair	1938
Billingham	Cleveland	St Cuthbert	Chairs, prie-dieu	1937-60
Bilsdale	Yorks.N	St John	Tapestry frame, litany desk	1936-45
Bingley	Yorks.W	Morton Hall, High Farnhill	Room panelling	1938
Birchencliff	Yorks.W	St Philip	Font cover	1948
Birdsall	Yorks.W	Churchyard	Memorial cross	1936
Birmingham	West Midlands	RC Cathedral	Kneehole desk	1929
Birstall	Yorks.W	St Peter	Large collection	
Bishop Auckland	Durham	St Helen	Altar candlesticks	1945
Bishop Wearmouth	Tyne & Wear	St Nicholas	Font	
Bishop's Sutton	Hampshire	Parish church	Furnishings	
Bishopthorpe	Yorks.N	St Andrew	Cross, carved figure of St George and dragon	1921-33
Bishopthorpe	Yorks.N	St Andrew	Font cover	
Blackburn	Lancs.	Well Church	Carved tablet	1937
Blackhall	Durham	Church	Reredos, panelling	1948
Blackpool	Lancs.	Holy Cross	Tables, stools	
Blackpool	Lancs.	Royal Oak Hotel	Panelling	1930
Blackpool	Lancs.	St Paul	Large collection	1938-48
Boltby	Yorks.N	Church	Reredos, panelling, altar rails	1946
Bolton	Gt. Manchester	Canon Slade Gram. Sch.	Platform table and chairs	
Bolton Abbey	Yorks.N	Church	Bishop's chair	1937-38
Bolton Percy	Yorks.N	All Saints	Lych gate, altar rail, candlesticks	1928-48
Bolton-le-Sands	Lancs.	United Ref.	Chairs	
Bolton-on-Swale	Yorks.N	St Mary	Tower screen	1935
Bossall	Yorks.N	Church	Lych gate	1912
Boston Spa	Yorks.W	Churchyard	Crosses	1938-42
Bowburn	Durham	Church	Altar, riddel posts	1948
Bracewell	Lancs.	St Michael	Pews	1972
Bradford	Yorks.W	Brad. Girls Grammar Sch.	Notice board, library furnishings	1936
Bradford	Yorks.W	Bradford Golf Club	Memorial panelling, doors	1932-36
Bradford	Yorks.W	City Hall	Lord Mayor's chair	
Bradford	Yorks.W	Fattorini and Gratten Off.s	Office furnishings	1930
Bradford	Yorks.W	Idle church	Litany desk	1946
Bradford	Yorks.W	Royal Infirmary	Tablet	1948
Bradford	Yorks.W	St Luke, Manningham	Processional cross	1941
Braeburn	Cumbria	Churchyard	Child's churchyard cross	1943
Brafferton	Durham	Vicarage	Desk	1948
Braithwell	Yorks.S	All Hallows	Various furnishings	
Bramhope	Yorks.W	Church	Panels, desks	1948
Bramhope	Yorks.W	St Giles	Panelling, cupboard, desks	1942
Bramley	Yorks.W	St Peter	Altar	1947
Bramshott	Hants	Parish church	Various furnishings	
Bramwith	Yorks.N	St Mary	Altar cross, table, reredos	1935
Brancepeth	Durham	St Brandon	Communion table	
Brandsby	Yorks.N	All Saints	Porch, seats, doors, panels	1913-32
Brantingham	Yorks.E	Parish church	Headstones	1945
Brecon	Powys	Cathedral	Screen	1963
Bridlington	Yorks.E	Christ Church	Pulpit, litany desk	1941
Bridlington	Yorks.E	Lords Feoffer	Tables, chairs	1934
Bridlington	Yorks.E	St Mary the Virgin Priory	Stalls, screens	1945-60
Brighouse	Yorks.W	St Chad	Memorial	
Brotton	Cleveland	Church	Altar rails, riddel posts	1933
Bubwith	Yorks.E	Church	Candlesticks, processional cross	1943-46
Bucknell	Shropshire	Church	Oak memorial	1932
Bulmer	Yorks.N	Church	Screen rebuild	1939
Bulwell	Notts.	St Mary	Reredos, tables	
Burghill	Hereford	St Mary	Floral stand	
Burley-in-Wharfedale	Yorks.W	St Mary	Large collection	1952-70
Burton Agnes	Yorks.E	St Martin	Staves, font, stand, stool	1979
Burton Salmon	Yorks.W		War memorial	1925
Buttercrambe	Yorks.E	Church	Altar	1930
Byrne	S.Africa		Offertory plate	
Cambridge	Cambs.	Emmanuel College	Bookrest	1937
Cambridge	Cambs.	Queen's College	Carved chest from Haileybury	1938
Cambridge	Cambs.	St Edmund's House	Refectory tables	1940
Cambridge	Cambs.	Trinity College	Tables, chairs, kneelers	1939
Canna	Hebrides	St Edward RC church	Communion rail	early
Carham	Northum.	Parish church	Altar, credence table	
Carleton-in-Craven	Yorks.N	St Mary	Choir stalls, altar rails	1950
Carlisle	Cumbria	Corby Castle	Large table	1937
Carlton Miniott	Yorks.N	St Laurence	Porch fittings, lych gate	1935
Castleford	Yorks.W	Castleford High School	Lectern	1972
Castleford	Yorks.W	Holy Cross, Airedale	Pews, benches, desk, kneelers	1934
Castleford	Yorks.W	Parish church	Rector's table	1946
Castleton	Yorks.N	St Michael & St George	Pews, screen, panelling, bench, desk	1935-39
Castletown	Caithness	St Clair Arms Hotel	Monk's chairs	
Catterick	Yorks.N	Royal Sig. Officers Mess	Tables, chairs, bench, bar fittings	1940
Catterick	Yorks.N	St Anne	Tower screen	1937
Catterick	Yorks.N	St Anne	Parclose screen	1937
Catterick Bridge	Yorks.N	Catterick Bridge Hotel	Dining tables, chairs, panelling fireplaces	1929-39
Catterick Camp	Yorks.N	Colburn Lodge	Screen, altar table, dias, cross, candlesticks, reredos	1947
Catterick Camp	Yorks.N	Officers Mess	Large collection of domestic items, panelling	1936
Catterick Camp	Yorks.N	Reg. Church St Aidan	Altar, bookcase, table, pulpit	1947
Catterick Camp	Yorks.N	St Martin Garrison Ch.	Missal stand	1944
Cheltenham	Glos.	The Green Dragon Inn	Full bar furnishings	1998
Chester	Cheshire	Cathedral	Notice boards	1946
Chichester	Sussex.W	Cathedral	Chest, trolleys, table, stands	
Chop Gate	Yorks.N	Church	Credence table, altar stand	1939
Chorley	Lancs.	Washington Hall T Col.	Lectern, carver chair	
Church Fenton	Yorks.N	St Mary	Paschal candlestick	
Cleckheaton	Yorks.W	Carlton House	Dining room complete	1932
Cleckheaton	Yorks.W	Methodist	Various furnishings	1962
Cleckheaton	Yorks.W	St John the Evangelist	Various furnishings	1965-72
Clitheroe	Lancs.	Waddow Hall (G.Guides)	Pew, prie-dieu	
Coalville	Leics.	Abbey	Missal stand	
Cobham	Surrey	Sandroyd School	Inscribed benches, panelling, kneelers	1930-35
Cockfield	Durham	Church	Stone War Memorial	1922
Codsall	Staffs	St Nicholas	Sanctuary chair	1938
Coedpoeth	Wrexham	St Tudfil	Sanctuary chair	1940
Coleman's Hatch	Sussex.E	Holy Trinity	Memorial plaque	1947
Colinton	Midlothian	St Cuthbert	Altar rails	
Collingham	Yorks.W	Church	Memorial door, seat	1948
Colne	Lancs.	Holy Trinity	Large collection	1950
Colton	Yorks.N	Church	Boards	1932
Colwinston	Glamorgan	St M & A Angels	Prie-dieu	1955
Conisbrough	Yorks.S	Clifton church	Desk, seat, pulpit	1947
Conistone	Yorks.N	St Mary	Furnishings	
Conway	Conwy	St Mary & St Michael	Altar rail	
Coopersale	Essex	St Albans	Pulpit	
Copmanthorpe	Yorks.N	Parish church	Sanctuary chairs	1936
Coventry	Warcs.	Cathedral	Enthronement chair	1943
Coverham	Yorks.N	Church	Credence table, font cover	1944-46
Coxhoe	Durham	Church	Credence table, desk, pulpit	1944-46
Coxwold	Yorks.N	Fauconberg Arms Inn	Bar, stools	
Coxwold	Yorks.N	St Michael	Large collection, lych gate	1923-40
Crambe	Yorks.N	St Michael	Memorial tablet and boards	1943-55
Cranwell	Lincs.	RAF	Tables	1927
Crathes	Aberdeenshire	Crathes Castle	Stool	
Crayke	Yorks.N	Rectory	Credence table	1948
Crichton	Midlothian	Parish church	Font	
Croft-on-Tees	Yorks.N	Croft Spa Hotel	Dining room furniture	
Crook	Durham	Church	Litany desk	1947
Cudworth	Yorks.S	St John the Baptist	Candlestick	1959
Cundall	Yorks.N	Cundall Manor School	Library furnishings	
Cundall	Yorks.N	Parish church	Churchyard gates	

Place	County	Building	Description	Date
Dacre	Yorks.N	Church	Screen, riddels, organ screen	1943
Dalton	Yorks.N	RAF Mess	Bars, overmantle	1944
Dalton	Yorks.N	St John	Altar rails	1933
Dalton	Yorks.N	St John	Churchyard gates	1937
Danby	Yorks.N	Church	Screens, stalls, altar, altar rails, desk	1925
Danby Wiske	Yorks.N	Parish church	Sanctuary & vestry furnishings	1943-69
Darlington	Durham	College of Education	Various furnishings	
Darlington	Durham	St Cuthbert	Bishop's chair	
Darlington	Durham	St Mark	Altar	
Darlington	Durham	St Paul	Chancel screen	1947
Darrington	Yorks.W	Church	Processional cross, tablet	1947
Dean	Cumbria	St Oswald	Large collection	1967-68
Deighton	Yorks.N	Church	Memorial chair	1948
Dewsbury	Yorks.W	Deaf and Dumb Inst.	Chair, alms dish, altar repairs	1936-48
Dodworth	Yorks.S	Church	Pulpit, choir stalls	1942-44
Doncaster	Yorks.S	Brodsworth church	Lectern	1943
Dormanstown	Cleveland	All Saints	Gable cross, shield	1931-42
Dorton	Bucks.	Ashford School	Refectory tables and chairs	
Drax	Yorks.N	Grammar school	Refectory tables, chairs, library furniture	1940
Drax	Yorks.N	Parish church	Tower screen	1938
Driffield	Yorks.E	Church	Prayer desk	1946
Drybergh	Borders	Dryberg Abbey Hotel	The Mouse Room	
Drypool	Yorks.E	St John	Candlesticks, kneelers, chapel furnishings	1934
Dunnington	Yorks.E	St Nicholas	Chantry chapel	1929
Durham	Durham	Belmont	Altar, reredos, panels, rails	1934
Durham	Durham	Cathedral	Restoration, clockcase, credence table	1934-41
Durham	Durham	Church	Churchyard gates	1937
Durham	Durham	County cricket club	Board	
Durham	Durham	Durham Castle	Lectern in chapel	
Durham	Durham	Durham School	Altar rails	1935
Durham	Durham	Hatfield College	Lectern in chapel	1948
Durham	Durham	St Chad's College SCR	Tables, chairs, panelling, monk's chair	1934-36
Durham	Durham	St Giles	Screen	1938-41
Durham	Durham	St Mary's College	Dining hall furniture	
Durham	Durham	Three Tuns	Bedroom furniture	1938
Durham	Durham	Ushaw College	Large kneeler, prie-dieu, tables	1937-57
Durham	Durham	Church	Candlesticks, altar	1944-48
Easby	Yorks.N	Church	Tablet	1948
Easington	Cleveland	All Saints	Screens, altar, crucifix	1934
Easingwold	Yorks.N	All Saints & John the Baptist	Screens, altars, panelling, prie-dieu	1937-48
Easingwold	Yorks.N	Grammar school	Chair, lectern	1947
East Grinstead	Sussex.W	St Mary	Pulpit	1942
East Grinstead	Sussex.W	St Swithen	Church doors, credence table	1926
East Harlsey	Yorks.N	Church	Litany desk, pulpit, bookrest, table	1927-47
East Keswick	Yorks.W	Parish	Priest's stall	
East Malling	Kent	St James	Altar rails	
East Preston	Sussex.W	Our Lady Star of Sea	Lectern	1966
East Witton	Yorks.N	St John the Evangelist	Pulpit, chest	1938-48
Ostend	Canada	St Augustine	Table	
Eberston	Yorks.N	Church	Seat	1948
Edinburgh	Lothian	St Mary (St Margaret)	Various furnishings	1924
Eccup	Yorks.W	St Mary	Altar and restoration	1936-38
Edbridge	Worcs.	Church	Altar cross	1938
Egington	Yorks.N	Holy Trinity	Screen, altar, riddel posts	1948
Emley	Yorks.W	St Michael	Porch door, gates	1970
Emsworth	Hants	St James	Small reader's stool	
Eston	Cleveland	St Chad	Litany desk, altar, reredos, dias, screen	1942-45
Exmouth	Northumberland	Church	Staves	1940
Fairfield	Derbys.	St Peter	Staves	1941
Farwater	Wales.S	St Peter	Font cover, choir stalls	
Farne Islands	Northum.	St Cuthbert	Cross, candlesticks	1933
Farnley	Yorks.W	Parish church	Bishop's chair, font cover	1935
Felixkirk	Yorks.N	St Felix	Lectern, altar, gates, candlesticks, table	1929-46
Flaxton	Yorks.N	Church	Furnishings	1947
Fleetwood	Lancs.	Rossall School	Table	
Fort Augustus	Highlands	St Benedict's Abbey	Choir screen	1923
Frampton-on-Severn	Glos.	Frampton Court	Collection of domestic furniture	
Frizington	Cumbria	St Joseph	Altar rails	1934
Fryston	Yorks.W	St Peter's	Kneelers	1934
Garstang	Lancs.	Chequered Flag Restaurant	Dining room furniture	
Garstang	Lancs.	New Hotel, Nateby	Tables, chairs	1930
Gawber	Yorks.S	Parish church	Panelling, seating, bookcase	
Giggleswick	Yorks.N	Woodlands Guest House	Furnishings	
Gilling West	Yorks.N	Churchyard	Cross	1938
Glasgow	Strathclyde	Scotstoun Shipyard	Roll of honour boards	1946
Goathland	Yorks.N	Church	Altar, doors, panelling, altar rails, reredos	1934-39
Gomersal	Yorks.W	Grove United Ref. church	Communion table, cross	1948-57
Goole	Yorks.E	Church	Chairs, stools	1948
Goole	Yorks.E	Church	Memorial gate	1938
Grahamstown	S.Africa	Cathedral	Memorial plaques	
Great Harrowden	Northants.	All Saints	Screen	1940
Great Smeaton	Yorks.N	Church	Pulpit, hymn boards	1948
Greenhow Hill	Yorks.N	Parish church	Gates, chapel furnishing	1948
Grinkle Park	Yorks.N	Grinkle Park Hotel	Bedsteads, chests, mantle shelf	1930-38
Grinton	Yorks.N	Grinton Church	Tablet	1944
Grosmont	Yorks.N	St Matthew	Altar	
Gt Ouseburn	Yorks.N	Church	Roof, bell frames, screen	1914-21
Gyffin	Conwy	St Benedict	Choir stalls, pulpit	1954
Haigh	Lancs.	Church	Large statue	1922
Halifax	Yorks.W	All Saints	Music stand	
Halifax	Canada	Cathedral	Pulpit	
Hampstead	London	St Mary, Hampstead	Kneelers, pews	1945
Hampsthwaite	Yorks.N	Parish church	Lych gate and collection	1938-47
Harlow Hill	Yorks.N	Church	Pulpit, lectern, stalls, altar rails	1940
Harome	Yorks.N	St Saviour	Communion rails	1911
Harome	Yorks.N	The Star Inn	Bar furnishings, fireplace	1934-48
Harrogate	Yorks.N	Austin Reed shop	Monk's chairs, dressing mirrors	
Harrogate	Yorks.N	Avenue Hotel	Tables, chairs, sideboard, chest	1938
Harrogate	Yorks.N	Beckwithshaw church	Font cover, litany desk	1948
Harrogate	Yorks.N	Christ church	Memorial rails	1936
Harrogate	Yorks.E	Dist. & Gen. Hospital	Nurses' home chapel furnishings	1930
Harrogate	Yorks.N	Harlow Hill	Altar rails	1946
Harrogate	Yorks.N	Harrogate College	Organ screen, choir stalls, lectern	1938
Harrogate	Yorks.N	Hospital Chapel	Various furnishings	1937-38
Harrogate	Yorks.N	South Stainley Church	Altar	1944
Harrogate	Yorks.N	St Mary	Sanctuary chair, altar rails	1946
Harrogate	Yorks.N	St Peter	Litany desk	1944
Harrogate	Yorks.N	St Robert	Board	1936
Harrogate	Yorks.N	St Wilfrid	Table, kneelers	1936-46
Harrogate	Yorks.N	St Wilfrid	Choir stalls, table, kneeler, reredos	1943
Harrogate	Yorks.N	Stonefall Cemetary chapel	Furnishings	1936
Harrogate	Yorks.N	Victoria Park Methodist	Altar, cross	1947
Harrogate	Yorks.N	Yorks. Agric. Soc.	Chairman's chair	
Hartlepool	Cleveland	Blackhall	Altar, candlesticks, cross	1945-46
Hartlepool	Cleveland	St Hilda	Bapistry seat	1948
Hartlepool	Cleveland	St Luke	Sanctuary chairs, reredos, panelling, screen	1947
Hatfield	Herts	Queenswood Girls Sch.	Chapel benches	
Haughton-le-Skerne	Durham	St Andrew	Altar rails	
Haverfordwest	Pembs.	St Mary	High altar	
Hawling	Glos.	Church	Altar, altar rails	1941
Headingley	Yorks.W	Methodist church	Communion table, lectern, kneelers	1937
Headingley	Yorks.W	St Michael	Desks, screens, kneelers	1938-47
Hebden Bridge	Yorks.W	St John	Bishop's chair, prie-dieu, font alms dish	1935

Helmsley	Yorks.N	All Saints	Altar table, kneelers, screen	1930-45
Helmsley	Yorks.N	Castle	Staircase	1927
Helmsley	Yorks.N	Cemetery	Gates, rails	1929
Helmsley	Yorks.N	National Park Office	Conservation award plaques	
Hillingdon	Herts.	Parish church	Altar	1938
Hillington	Norfolk	Uphall	Altar	
Hitchin	Herts.	Girls' Grammar School	Table	
Hitchin	Herts.	St Mary	Altar and rails	1952
Hoddlesden	Lancs.	St Paul	Reredos, altar cross	1948
Holbeck	Yorks.W	St Matthew	Chapel furnishings	1932
Hollinwood	Lancs.	Church	Sanctuary table, credence table	1947
Holloway	Derbys.	Christ Church	Flower pedestal	
Holme-on-Spalding Moor	Yorks.E	All Saints	Screen, various furnishings	1938-45
Holtby	Yorks.N	Holy Trinity	Organ stool, priest stall, lectern, kneeler	1937-38
Holy Island	Northum.	Church	Table, bookends, crosses	1940
Hope	Derbys.	St Peter	Choir stalls	
Hornsea	Yorks.E	Church	Children's chairs, candlesticks	1936
Horsehouse	Yorks.N	Church	Credence table	1946
Horsforth	Yorks.W	Church	Screens, tablets	1920-21
Hovingham	Yorks.N	Church	Altar, candlesticks	1937
Hovingham	Yorks.N	Hovingham Hall	Memorial tablet	1937-48
Howden	Yorks.E	St Peter Minster	Furnishings	1932-47
Howsham	Yorks.N	Church	Gates	1948
Hoyland	Yorks.S	Sacred Heart & St Helen	Circular-backed chair	1929
Hubberholme	Yorks.N	St Michael & All Angels	Pews, stalls, seats, desks, bowls	1933-34
Huddersfield	Yorks.W	Holy Trinity	Tall candlesticks, board, credence table	1944
Huddersfield	Yorks.W	Royds Mount School	Lectern and chairs	1949
Huddersfield	Yorks.W	St Peter	Mem.screen, altar, table, chairs	1944-48
Huddersfield	Yorks.W	Almondbury	Pulpit crucifix, tablet	1948
Huddersfield	Yorks.W	St David Prep. School	Prayer desk	1948
Huddersfield	Yorks.W	United Ref. Moldgreen	Lectern, font, chairs	
Hull	Yorks.E	Andrew Marvell H. Sch.	Lectern	1969
Hull	Yorks.E	Anlaby St Peter	Altar	1938
Hull	Yorks.E	Bishop of Hull	Bishop's staff and case	1945
Hull	Yorks.E	Holy Trinity	South door, screen, desks	1936-46
Hull	Yorks.E	St John's church	Wrought iron chancel gates	1932
Hull	Yorks.E	St John's Vicarage	Fireplace, kneelers, candlesticks	1934
Hunmanby	Yorks.N	Hunmanby Hall School	Refectory table, chairs	1930
Huntington	Yorks.N	St Andrew	Kneelers, lectern, desks, cross	1939-47
Husthwaite	Yorks.N	St Nicholas	Miscellaneous collection	1920-47
Husthwaite	Yorks.N	Wesleyan	Communion chair and table	1928
Hutton Buscel	Yorks.N	St Matthias	Litany desk, kneelers, stalls	1936-40
Hutton Magna	Durham	Church	Lych gate	1920
Hutton Rudby	Yorks.N	Church	Lych gate	1932
Hutton-le-Hole	Yorks.N	St Chad	Altar rails, reredos	1934
Hythe	Kent	Sch. of Inf., Marlsford	Lectern, dias	1948
Ickham	Kent	Church	Tablet	1935
Ilkley	Yorks.W	All Saints	Organ cases, various	1953
Ilkley	Yorks.W	St Margaret	Altar rails, candlesticks, chairs, bishop's chair	1934-41
Ilmington	Warcs.	St Mary	Vast collection	1938-39
Ingleby Arncliffe	Yorks.N	All Saints	Altar rails	1926
Ingleton	Yorks.N	St Mary	Altar, altar rails, cross, candlesticks	
Isle of Ensay	Hebrides	Private chapel	Door	
Kelloe	Durham	St Helen	Altar	1925-29
Kepwick	Yorks.N	Church	Hymn board	1938
Kepwick	Yorks.N	Kepwick Hall	Entrance gates	1935
Kepwick	Yorks.N	Kepwick Hall	Pulpit, altar rails, kneeler, priest stall, credence table	1946
Keswick	Cumbria	Church	Sanctuary chair, stools	1928
Kettlewell	Yorks.N	Manor House	Collection	1938
Kettlewell	Yorks.N	St Mary's	Panelling	1937
Kidderminster	Worcs.	Town Hall	Refectory table	
Kilburn	Yorks.N	Forresters' Arms	Bar furnishings	
Kilburn	Yorks.N	St Mary	Large collection	1925-40
Kilburn	Yorks.N	Village	War memorial, seat	1921-40
Kildwick	Yorks.N	Farnhill Manor	Domestic furnishings	
Kildwick	Yorks.N	St Andrew	Candlesticks	
Killinghall	Yorks.N	Church	Screen	1938
Kings Lynn	Norfolk	Church	Altar	1937
Kingswinsford	West Midlands	Holy Trinity	Pair of gates	
Kirby Knowle	Yorks.N	St Wilfrid	Staves, panelling	1935-38
Kirby Misperton	Yorks.N	Church	Inscribed panel, altar rails	1931-44
Kirby Overblow	Yorks.N	Church	Altar, table, stools	1940-47
Kirby Wiske	Yorks.N	Church	Altar rails, credence table, lych gate, organ front, war memorial	1919-23
Kirk Bramwith	Yorks.S	St Mary	Altar, altar rail, pulpit, pews, stalls, lectern	1936-48
Kirk Ella	Yorks.E	Parish church	Carved and inscibed cross	1942
Kirk Hammerton	Yorks.N	Church	Reredos	1947
Kirk Merrington	Durham	Church	Font cover	1937
Kirkby Fleetham	Yorks.N	The Hall	Kneelers	1949
Kirkby Malham	Yorks.N	St Michael & James	Octagonal table	1937
Kirkby Malzeard	Yorks.N	St Andrew	Chairs, candlesticks, cross	1937-38
Kirkby	Yorks.N	St Augustine	Chair	1948
Kirkdale	Yorks.N	St Gregory's Minster	Sanctuary chair	1937
Kirklevington	Cleveland	St Martin	Screen, surplice press	1936
Knaresborough	Yorks.N	St John	Altar chest, board, gospel lights	1944
Lanchester	Durham	All Saints	Pews, boards, font, table	1939
Langthwaite	Yorks.N	St Mary the Virgin	Reredos, altar	
Langton	Yorks.N	St Andrew	Panelling behind pulpit	1935-38
Lechlade	Glos.	Southrop Manor	Large table	1930
Leeds	Yorks.W	All Hallows St Simon	Stalls, altar rails	1962
Leeds	Yorks.W	All Saints	Cross, candlesticks, riddel posts	1938-9
Leeds	Yorks.W	Bishop's House	Kneelers, chairs	1939
Leeds	Yorks.W	Burmantofts St Agnes	Altar table, angels, altar rails	1936
Leeds	Yorks.W	Civic Hall	Bookcase	1948
Leeds	Yorks.W	Cockburn High School	Lectern	
Leeds	Yorks.W	Cross Flatts Park School	Tablet	1948
Leeds	Yorks.W	Girls' High School	Library furnishings	1933-37
Leeds	Yorks.W	Grammar school	Choir stalls	1933
Leeds	Yorks.W	Middleton St Cross	Chancel furnishings	1935
Leeds	Yorks.W	School of Medicine	Staffroom furniture	1936
Leeds	Yorks.W	St Margaret	Altar, desk	1945
Leeds	Yorks.W	TOC H, Brotherton House	Altar cross	1936
Leeds	Yorks.W	Wesley College	Chancel chairs	1934
Leeds	Yorks.W	Woodlesford Church	Rails, lectern	1948
Leeds	Yorks.W	Wortley St John the Evan.	Reredos	1948
Leeds	Yorks.W	Yorks. Archeo. Society	Rocking cradle	1939
Leeds	Yorks.W	Yorks. Copper Works	Tables, chairs, trolley, wine cupboard	1939
Leeds	Yorks.W	Convent Little Sisters of Poor	Furnishings	
Leeming	Yorks.N	RAF Station Officers Mess	Furnishings, altar rails, litany desk, cross, candlesticks	1941
Leeming	Yorks.N	WRAF Offi. Mess	Furnishings	1941
Leeming Bar	Yorks.N	Dale Pack Food Ltd.	Boardroom table, chair, cupboard	
Leicester	Leics.	Grand Hotel	Pews in Simon's bar	
Leicester	Leics.	Ratcliffe College	Refectory tables and chairs	
Leicester	Leics.	St Mary	Desk	1939
Levisham	Yorks.N	Church	Pews, benches, altar rails, lectern	1946
Leyburn	Yorks.N	St Mary Mount	Altar rails	1936
Leyburn	Yorks.N	St Matthew	Lectern, pulpit, prie-dieu, font cover	1940-46
Leyburn	Yorks.N	St Peter and Paul	Altar rails	1936
Leyland	Lancs.	St Mary	Doors, pulpit, pews	
Lindley	Yorks.W	Church	Lectern	1948
Linton	Yorks.W	Woodhall Centre	Tables, benches, candlesticks	
Lisburn	N. Ireland	Church	Credence table	
Liverpool Sefton	Merseyside	St Helen	Carvings	
Liverpool Waterloo	Merseyside	St Mary the Virgin	Altar, reredos and altar rails	1936
Llanallgo	Anglesey	Church	Desks, seats	1934
Llandinam	Powys	Broneirion GG Centre	Refectory tables, benches	
Llandudno	Gwynedd	Holy Trinity	Screen	
Llanllywel	Gwent	St Llywell	Furnishings	
Loftus	Cleveland	St Leonard	Kneeler	1933
Londesborough	Yorks.E	Rectory	Processional cross	1946

Place	County	Building	Items	Date
London	London	Austin Reed shop	Monk's chairs, dressing mirrors	
London	London	Ben Johnson Printers	Boardroom tables & monks' chairs	
London	London	Church Ho. Westminster	Octagonal burr table	
London	London	Hackney Wick	Sanctuary stools	1944
London	London	Haileybury College	Tables, benches, chairs, gong stand	1933-36
London	London	Imp. Canc. Research Cen	Bookcase	
London	London	London Ho. Bloomsbury	Large tables	1937
London	London	Royal Oceanic Racing Club	Bar stools, furnishings	1936-42
London	London	Wax Chandlers' Hall	Lectern, rose bowl stand	
London	London	Westminster Abbey	Credence table, candlesticks	1941-42
London	London	Westminster Cathedral	Credence table	1937
London Fulham	London	All Saints	Clergy stalls	
London Mill Hill	London	St Paul	Prayer desks	
London Warwick St.	London	Church	Table	
Long Marston	Yorks.N	Church	Tablet	1948
Longton	Lancs.	St Andrew	Altar, cross, chests, panel	
Longwood	Yorks.S	St Mark	Stools, lectern	1949
Lothersdale	Yorks.N	Christ Church	Entrance door	1938
Lothersdale	Yorks.N	Lothersdale Rectory	Church door	1938
Lupset	Yorks.S	Church	Litany desk	1947
Lytham St Annes	Lancs.	St Cuthbert	Memorial gates	1966-72
Malton	Yorks.N	Grammar school	Tablet	1939
Malton	Yorks.N	Green Man Hotel	Complete bar furnishings	1935-42
Malton	Yorks.N	St Michael & St Leonard	Stalls, screen, altar, reredos, riddels	1920-45
Malton	Yorks.N	Wesleyan Chapel	Furnishings	1947
Malton Old	Yorks.N	St Mary's Priory	Door, pulpit, lectern, panelling	1931-38
Malvern Link	Worcs.	St Matthias	Screen, candlesticks	1935-40
Manchester	Gt. Manchester	Middleton Rectory	Pastoral staff	1944
Market Weighton	Yorks.E	Church	Choir stalls, kneelers	1941
Marlesford	Suffolk	St Andrew	Lectern	
Martindale	Cumbria	St Peter	Entrance gate	
Marton	Cleveland	Marton Grove	Coffin stools, altar rails, missal stand	1935-42
Marton	Cleveland	St Cuthbert	Priest's stalls, prayer desk	1947
Mayland	Essex	Church	Credence table	1929
Melton Mowbray	Leics.	St Mary	Reredos, altar rails, altar, desk, seats	1925-29
Menston	Yorks.W	St John the Divine	Various furnishing	1948
Methil	Fife	Church	Organ case, screens, stalls,	1925
Methley	Yorks.W	St Oswald	Tower screen, altar rails	1928-48
Middlesbrough	Middlesbrough	Marton Grove	Altar, kneelers, pulpit, seats, candlesticks	1934
Middlesbrough	Cleveland	South Bank	Panelling, reredos	1937-42
Middlesbrough	Cleveland	St Cuthbert	Gates	1932
Middlesbrough	Cleveland	St Joseph	Celebrant's chair, candlestick	1939
Middlesbrough	Cleveland	St Luke	Notre Dame devil carving	1932
Middlesbrough	Cleveland	St Oswald Grove Hill	Furnishings	1934
Middlesbrough	Cleveland	St Thos.Brambles Farm	Altar, lectern	1944-45
Middleton Tyas	Yorks.N	St Michael & All Angels	Altar, altar rails	
Midhope	Yorks.S	St James the Less	Flower stand	
Millington	Yorks.E	Church	Kneelers, crosss	1942
Milnsbridge	Yorks.W	Baptist chapel	Communion table, altar, chairs	1936
Milnsbridge	Yorks.W	St Luke	Panelling, candlesticks	1931
Mirfield	Yorks.W	Battyeford Church	Altar cross, candlesticks	1947
Mirfield	Yorks.W	Sion Baptist	Lectern	1950
Moffat	Dumfries.	St John the Evangelist	Altar	1951
Moniac Castle	Inverness	Private RC chapel	Kneelers, chairs	1933-38
Monkwearmouth	Tyne & Wear	All Saints	Lectern, episcopal chair	1942-44
Morecambe	Lancs.	Christ Church	Font, cross	1964
Morecambe	Lancs.	Girl Guide Assoc.	Flagpole	
Mottram-Longdendale	Cheshire	St Michael	Altar rail	
Mountain Ash	Rhondda Cynon Taff	St Margaret	Altar rails, credence table	
Muker	Yorks.N	St Mary	Lectern	
Mytholmroyd	Yorks.W	St Michael	Statuette	
N. Otterington	Yorks.N	Church	Reredos repairs	1924
Nairn	Highlands	St Andrew	Reredos, panelling, altar rails	1936-47
Narborough	Leics.	All Saints	Reredos, crucifix, candlesticks	
Nawton	Yorks.N	Kirkdale Church	Sanctuary chair	1946
Nevilles Cross	Durham	St John	Pews, rood screen	1935-37
New Addington	Surrey	St Edward-t-K&C	Furnishing	1958
New Brighton	Merseyside	All Saints	Bapistry seats	1928
New Ollerton	Notts.	St Joseph	Lady altar, seating	1929-43
Newburgh	Yorks.N	Newburgh Priory School	Pews	1944
Newby	Yorks.N	St Mark	Lectern	
Newcastle-u-Tyne	Tyne & Wear	Cathedral St Nicholas	St George's chapel complete	1939
Newcastle-u-Tyne	Tyne & Wear	Dame Allan's School	Lectern	1950
Newcastle-u-Tyne	Tyne & Wear	Rutherford Gr. School	Memorial lectern	1948
Newcastle-u-Tyne	Tyne & Wear	St John	Complete lady chapel	1936-37
Newport	Gwent	Cathedral St Woolos	Canon's stalls	
Newton Green	Suffolk	All Saints	Candlesticks	
Nigg	Ross	Parish church	Altar, altar rails, candlesticks, missal stand	1936
Normanton	Yorks.W	All Saints	Curate's stall, priest's stall	1938
Normanton	Yorks.W	St Mary	Font cover	1939
North Cave	Yorks.E	Church	Church door	1940
North Grimston	Yorks.N	Church	Gospel lights	1946
North Shields	Tyne & Wear	Northumberland Square	Carved 'Wooden Dolly'	
North Shields	Tyne & Wear	St Peter	Processional cross, alms dish	1938
Northallerton	Yorks.N	All Saints	Altar rails, memorial, seat, Lady chapel furnishings	1931-48
Northallerton	Yorks.N	Methodist	Display table	
Norton	Yorks.N	Methodist	Seating	
Norton	Yorks.N	St Peter	Altar, reredos, pews, stool	1937-48
Norton-on-Tees	Cleveland	St Mary the Virgin	Lych gate, pews, chairs	1948
Norton-on-Tees	Cleveland	St Michael & All Angels	Panelling, screen	1934
Nossmayo	Devon	Parish church	Pews	
Nottingham	Notts.	Bluecoat School	Lectern, board, table, chairs	
Nottingham	Notts.	RC Cathedral	Kneelers	1933
Nottingham	Notts.	St Barnabas Cathedral	Prie-dieu	1939
Nottingham	Notts.	St Peter	Font cover	
Nunburnholme	Yorks.E	St James	Altar rails	1946
Nunnington	Yorks.N	All Saints & St James	Lectern, screen, riddels,	1929-46
Nunthorpe	Cleveland	St Mary	Altar, kneeler, dias, table, lych gate	1940-47
Old Byland	Yorks.N	The Green	Coronation seat	1937
Old Swinford	Worcs.	St Mary	Yard gates	1929
Oldham	Gt. Manchester	St Stephen	Altar rails	1946
Oldstead	Yorks.N	Black Swan	Alterations	1930-32
Ollerton	Notts.	Ollerton Hall	Altar, canopied reredos	1929
Osmondthorpe	Yorks.W	St Philip	Choir stalls, lectern, altar,	1930-46
Ossett	Yorks.W	Parish church	Organ stool, table, chair	1947
Oswaldkirk	Yorks.W	Church	Priest stall	1947
Otterington North	Yorks.N	Church	Reredos	1924
Otterington South	Yorks.N	St Andrew	Sanctuary panelling, vestry screen, collection table	1920-34
Owlston	Yorks.N	Church	Reredos	1937
Owston	Yorks.S	All Saints	Reredos	1938
Oxford	Oxon	Blackfriars	Bench	1933
Oxford	Oxon	Crown and Thistle	Octagonal tables	1938
Oxford	Oxon	Dashwood	Tablet	1947
Oxford	Oxon	Somerville College	Entrance doors	1934
Pannal	Yorks.N	St Robert of K	Tables, notice board	1936
Pateley Bridge	Yorks.N	Church	Altar, cross, altar rails, credence table	1936
Patterdale	Cumbria	St Patrick	Church warden staves	1920-30
Peacehaven	Sussex E	Peacehaven Hotel	Dining room chairs, tables	
Penmaenmawr	Gwynedd	St Seiriol	Altar, screen	
Peterborough	Cambridgeshire	Cathedral	Refectory table, cupboards	1949
Peterhead	Aberdeenshire	St Peter	Reredos	1926
Pickering	Yorks.N	Church	Font cover	1946
Piercebridge	Durham	George Hotel	Various furnishings	1935
Pluscarden	Moray	Priory of Our Lady	Choir stalls	
Pocklington	Yorks.E	All Saints	Altar rails	1926

Place	County	Church/Institution	Items	Date
Pool-in-Wharfedale	Yorks.W	Methodist	Pulpit, reredos, communion table, altar rail	1937-55
Pool-in-Wharfedale	Yorks.W	St Wilfrid	Reredos, tablet	1938-48
Pott Shrigley	Cheshire	St Christopher	Porch door	
Potten End	Herts.	Holy Trinity	Lectern, choir stalls	
Priorslee	Shropshire	St Peter	Bishop's seat, prie-dieu	1959
Ramsgill	Yorks.N	Church	West doors	1947
Ratcliffe-on-Wreake	Leics.	Ratcliffe College	Refectory tables, chairs	1937-38
Reading	Berks.	London Police Fed. HQ	Chairman's chair	
Reculver	Kent	St Mary	Organ case	
Redcar	Cleveland	Borough Council	Borough arms	1948
Redcar	Cleveland	Sacred Heart	Bishop's chair	
Redcar	Cleveland	St Peter	Panelling, chair, reredos	1936-39
Redmarshall	Cleveland	Church	Lych gate	1948
Redmire	Yorks.N	St Mary	Pulpit, lectern	1947
Retford	Notts.	Ranby House Prep. Sch.	Completely panelled dormitory	
Richmond	Yorks.N	Green Howard Museum	Large collection	1938-40
Richmond	Yorks.N	Gunnerside Lodge	Oak room	1930-1931
Richmond	Yorks.N	Kings Hotel and Cafe	Fireplace and beams	1929
Richmond	Yorks.N	Regimental chapel	Large collection of items	1932-39
Richmond	Yorks.N	St Mary the Virgin	Large collection	1933-45
Rievaulx	Yorks.N	Church	Carved figures	1932
Ripon	Yorks.N	Cathedral	Tall candlesticks, pulpit	1937-47
Ripon	Yorks.N	Grammar school	Lectern	
Ripon	Yorks.N	St Margaret	Stalls	1934
Ripon	Yorks.N	Training college	Alms box	1934-38
Ripponden	Yorks.W	St Bartholomew	Font cover	
Rochester	Kent	Rochester Bridge Chapel	Tables, chairs	1938
Romaldkirk	Durham	St Ronald	Reredos, panelling, angels, riddel posts	1937-38
Rosedale	Yorks.N	Church	Seating	1909
Rothwell	Lincs.	Church	Stall backs	1947
Roundhay	Yorks.W	St Andr. Uni. R. Roundhay	Five chairs	
Royton	Gt. Manchester	St Anne	Lectern	1936
Ruswarp	Yorks.N	Church	Rood beam, cross and figure	1920
St Albans	Herts.	United Reform	Font	1955
St John's Chapel	Durham	Church	Panelling, table, altar, altar rails	1911
St John's Wood	Bucks.	All Saints	Screen, altar rails, table	1939-40
Sth. Kilvington	Yorks.N	Church	Oak table	1926
Sale	Cheshire	AEI Hostel	Staircase	
Salford	Gt. Manchester	Bishop Chapel	Alterations	1933
Sand Hutton	Yorks.N	St Leonards	Reredos, panelling, stalls	1913-38
Scarborough	Yorks.N	Church	Dish, candlesticks, crosses, credence table	1932
Scarborough	Yorks.N	Cricket Club House	Refectory table, sideboard, chairs	1950
Scarborough	Yorks.N	Prince of Wales Hotel	Beds	1936
Scarborough	Yorks.N	Queen Margaret's school	Tables and chairs with carving	1938
Scarborough	Yorks.N	St Columba	Sounding board, missals stand	1938-44
Scarborough	Yorks.N	St James	Various furnishings	
Scarborough	Yorks.N	St Luke	Table, prayer desks, staves	1933-44
Scarborough	Yorks.N	St Martin	Memorial	1938
Sculcoates	Yorks.E	St Mary	Pews	1934-36
Sculcoates	Yorks. E	St Patrick chapel	Various furnishings	1934
Seaford	Sussex.E	School	Memorial tables	1948
Seaford	Sussex E	St Peter	Lectern	1947
Seamer	Yorks.N	Church	Cross, altar	1944
Seamer-in-Cleveland	Cleveland	St Martin	Church door, altar, rails	1944
Seaton	Cumbria	St Paul	Choir stalls, prie-dieu, pulpit	
Seaton Carew	Cleveland	Holy Trinity	Rails, priest stall	1939-48
Selby	Yorks.N	Abbey St Mary & Germ.	Stall canopies, altar	1938-55
Selby	Yorks.N	Coach Ho. Gateforth Hall	Monumental kitchen dresser	
Settrington	Yorks.N	All Saints	Reredos, altar rails, panelling, pulpit	1922-25
Settrington	Yorks.N	All Saints	Litany desk, organ seat	1937-47
Settrington	Yorks.N	All Saints	Screen	1923
Settrington	Yorks.N	All Saints	Doors	1925
Settrington	Yorks.N	All Saints	Staves	1926
Settrington	Yorks.N	All Saints	Gates for churchyard	1927
Settrington	Yorks.N	All Saints	Litany desk	1927
Settrington	Yorks.N	All Saints	Alms box	1929
Shadwell	Yorks.W	Shadwell Church	Pulpit, stalls, altar rails, lectern, display case	1947
Shepton Mallet	Somerset	All Hallows	Lectern	1968
Sherborne	Dorset	Sherborne Prep. School	Refectory table, chairs	
Shirley	Hants	Roman Catholic church	Entrance doors	
Shirley	West Midlands	TSB College, Monkspath	Lectern	
Shotley Bridge	Durham	St Cuthbert	Credence table	1937
Sicklinghall	Yorks.N	Immaculate Conception	Various furnishing	1950-68
Sicklinghall	Yorks.N	Parish church	Lectern	1942
Skeffling	Yorks.E	Church	Bosses	1936
Skipton	Yorks.N	High Farnhill	Hall panelling, fireplace, staircase	1937
Skipton	Yorks.N	Christ Church	Altar, reredos	
Skipton	Yorks.N	Holy Trinity	Bookcase	1956
Skipton	Yorks.N	The Council Chamber	Various furnishing	
Skipton-on-Swale	Yorks.N	RCAF Station	Bar	1944
Skipton-on-Swale	Yorks.N	Skipton Bridge church	Memorial, sanctuary chair	1921-45
Slingsby	Yorks.N	All Saints	Plaque, tablet, table	1947
Slough	Berks.	Horlicks	Board room, office furniture	1925-38
Slough	Berks.	ICI Paints Division	Dining tables, chairs	
Snainton	Yorks.N	Church	Chair	1936
South Bank	Cleveland	Parish church	Door, panelling, reredos	1937-44
South Cave	Yorks.E	Parish church	Memorial cross, door	1939-44
South Kirkby	Yorks.W	Church	Sanctuary candlesticks, stool	1943-44
South Milford	Yorks.N	St Mary	Pulpit	1950
South Moor	Durham	St George	Furnishing	1938
South Shields	Durham	St Hilda	Font cover	1948
Southport	Merseyside	King George V School	Tablets	1948
Southwell	Notts.	St Mary Minster	Various furnishings	
Southwold	Suffolk	St Edmund K & Martyr	Bookcase, cupboard	
Spalding	Lincs.	St John the Baptist	Large collection	1938-46
Spalding	Lincs.	Weston St Mary	Pulpit	1943
Spennithorne	Yorks.N	St Michael & All Angels	Reredos	1947
Spofforth	Yorks.N	All Hallows	Various furnishing	1955-56
Stainton	Cleveland	St Peter & Paul	Various furnishings	1972
Stanbrook	Worcs.	Abbey of St Mary	Various furnishings	1926-39
Standish	Lancs	St Nicholas	Priest's stall, desk stools, crosses	1922-30
Stanley	Durham	Church	Credence table, seating	1933-37
Stevenage	Herts.	St Nicholas	Pews	
Stillingfleet	Yorks.N	Parish church	Credence table	
Stillington	Cleveland	St Nicholas	Lectern, altar, floor, crucifix	1935-46
Stockton-on-Forest	Yorks.N	Holy Trinity	Chancel screen, tablet, stalls, altar rails	1923-38
Stockton-on-Tees	Cleveland	St Paul	Seat fronts, litany desk	1937-47
Stokesley	Yorks.N	St Peter & St Paul	Screen, doors, altar missal stands, altar rails	1939-48
Stonegrave	Yorks.N	Church	Sanctuary chair	1941
Stratford-upon-Avon	Warwickshire	Austin Reed shop	Fireplace, mirrors, dresser's chairs	
Streat	Sussex W	Parish church	Lectern	
Strensall	Yorks.N	Church	Lectern, tablet, pulpit, screen	1948
Stretton	Cheshire	Church	Tablet	1948
Sunderland	Tyne & Wear	Crematorium	Panels, pews	1938
Surbiton	Surrey	Wesleyan	Altar table	1932
Sutton-on-Derwent	Yorks.E	St Michael & All Angels	Seating, stalls	1928
Sutton-on-Forest	Yorks.N	Church	Altar rails, carved screens	1922
Sutton-on-Trent	Notts.	Church	Crucifix	1927
Swillington	Yorks.W	Church	Memorial cross	1921
Tadcaster	Yorks.N	RAF Kirkby Wharf	Altar cross, candlesticks	1941
Tain	Highlands	St Andrew	Reredos, altar rails, lectern	1936-67
Tamworth	Staffs.	St Joseph's Convent	Various furnishings	1932
Tan Hill	Yorks.N	Tan Hill Inn	Dining tables, chairs	1946
Tanfield	Yorks.N	Church	Chairs, sanctuary chair	1937-38
Tarleton	Lancs.	Holy Trinity	Chair, litany desk	1962
Tealby	Lincs.	All Saints	Candlesticks	1944
Terrington	Yorks.N	Church	Memorial gates	1947
Thaxted	Essex	St John the Baptist	Various furnishings	

Place	County	Location	Item	Date
...irkleby	Yorks.N	Church	Cross for roof, tablet, crosses	1928-48
...hirsk	Yorks.N	Rotary Club	Gavel, bookcase	1938
...hirsk	Yorks.N	St Mary	War memorial, board, candlesticks, shelf	1920-40
...horganby	Yorks.N	St Helen	Lych gate	1930
...hornaby-on-Tees	Cleveland	St Paul	Light holders	1936
...hornthwaite	Cumbria	Blessed Virgin Mary	Bishop's chair	
...hornton Watlass	Yorks.N	Private RC chapel	Altar, reredos	1933
...hornton-le-Dale	Yorks.N	All Saints	Memorial stone, prie-dieu, candlesticks	1920-45
...horp Arch	Yorks.W	All Saints	Various furnishings	1935-42
...icehurst	Sussex E	St Mary	Choir stalls, lectern	1961-64
...ideswell	Derbys.	St John the Baptist	Various furnishings	
...odmorden	Yorks.W	Grammar school	Table and chairs	1962
...ooting	Surrey	St George Hosp. chapel	Chairs	
...opcliffe	Yorks.N	Queen Mary's School	Bookcase, credence table, tables, chairs	1937-47
...oon	South Ayrshire	St Ninian	Door, bishop's chair, cupboard	1937-56
...nemouth	Tyne & Wear	St Augustin of Hippo	Choir stalls	
...ppingham	Rutland	Uppingham School	Tables, chairs, benches	1950-64
...psall	Yorks.N	Upsall Castle	Large oak staircase	1924
...SA	USA	NFS Fire Station	Plaque	1944
...akefield	Yorks.W	Cathedral All Saints	Large collection	1940-64
...akefield	Yorks.W	Girl's Grammar School	Carved tablet, plaque	1932-36
...akefield	Yorks.W	Lupset church	Prayer desk	1948
...akefield	Yorks.W	Pinderfields Hos. chapel	Various furnishings	
...akefield	Yorks.W	St Michael	Clergy seat, desk	1944
...altham	Lincs.	All Saints	Screen, aumbry door	1962
...arwick Bridge	Cumbria	Church	Altar rails	1948
...arton	Lancs.	St Oswald	Chairs	
...ass	Yorks.N	Mission chapel	Riddel posts and rail, lectern	1938-46
...atford	Herts.	Reeds School	Library	1940
...ell	Yorks.N	St Michael	Alms dishes, altar, kneelers, cross	1935-38
...ell	Yorks.N	Well Hall	Fireplaces	1931
...ells	Somerset	Cathedral	Gospel lights	1946
...ensley	Yorks.N	Church	Crucifix memorial	1947
...est Heslerton	Yorks.N	Church	Tablet	1947
...est Tanfield	Yorks.N	St Nicholas	Bishop's chairs	1934
...estleigh	Devon	St John the Baptist	Table, seating	1924
...eston	Yorks.N	All Saints	Porch door	
...eston	Lincs.	St Mary	Gospel lights	1947
...eston-on-Trent	Derbys	St Andrews	Altar rails	
...etherby	Yorks.W	Church	Tablet, table	1948
...henby	Yorks.N	Church	Pulpit	1922
...hitby	Yorks.N	Sneaton Castle	Chest, prayer desk, book cases, seats	1934-50
...hitby	Yorks.N	St Hilda's Priory	Prie-dieu, lectern, chairs, table	1934-45
...hitby	Yorks.N	St Hilda's School	Dining hall furnishings	
...hitley Bay	Northum.	Victoria Hotel	Long settle	1936
...hittington	Staffs.	Barracks	Octagonal table	1938
...ckwar	Glos.	Holy Trinity	Priest's stall	1930
...lsill	Yorks.N	Church	Altar rails	1938
...nchester	Hants	Cathedral	Kneelers	1933
...nchester	Hants	Winchester College	Tables and chairs	1933
...nkburn	Notts.	Church	Table	1935
...nksley	Yorks.N	St Cuthbert	Prie-dieu	1938
...nksley	Yorks.N	Winksley church	Litany desk	1938
...nsford	Somerset	Verdin Grammar School	Lectern	1949
...sbech	Cambs.	St Mary's	Notice board	1938
...stow	Yorks.N	All Saints	Screen, altar, altar rails, credence table	1936-38
...thington	Glos.	The Mill Inn	Furnishings	1932
...ttington	Berks.	Regimental Depot	Fender seat, monk's chair, coffee tables	1937
...king	Surrey	Golf Club	80 chairs, 17 tables	1992
...lverhampton	West Mid.	Girls' High School	Lectern and several chairs	
...lverhampton	West Mid.	St Peter Collegiate	Chairs	1948
...odkirk	Yorks.W	Parish	Prie-dieu	
...rkington	Cumbria	Our Lady & St Michael	Large collection	1921-22

Place	County	Location	Item	Date
Worksop	Notts	St Anne	Altar rails	1948
Worksop	Notts.	St Mary	Doors	
Worksop	Notts	Worksop College	Various refectory furniture	
Worthen	Shropshire	All Saints	Litany desk	
Wortley	Yorks.S	St Leonard	Credence table	
Wrexham	Wales.N	Maelor General Hospital	Altar rail	
Wycliffe	Durham	St Mary	Altar rail, choir stalls, pulpit, pews	1948-50
Wykeham	Yorks.N	St Helen & All Saints	Various furnishings	1936-48
Yarm	Cleveland	Church	Altar rails	1948
Yarm	Cleveland	Grammar school	Lectern, tablet	1948
Yearsley	Yorks.N	Parish church	Pulpit	1909
York	Yorks.N	All Saints, Pavement	Organ case, panelling, litany desk, riddels	1931-63
York	Yorks.N	Austin Reed shop	Monk's chairs, dressing mirrors	
York	Yorks.N	Ben Johnson Printers	Boardroom tables & monks' chairs	
York	Yorks.N	College for Girls	Inscribed table	1938
York	Yorks.N	Dringhouses church	Stone memorial, altar rails, chairs, table, stools	1921-41
York	Yorks.N	Farlington church	Credence table	1943
York	Yorks.N	Guildhall	Refectory table, memorial seats	1944-57
York	Yorks.N	Holy Redeemer	Board	1938
York	Yorks.N	Library	Outside seats inscribed	1946
York	Yorks.N	Medical Society	Rostrum, gavel	1933
York	Yorks.N	Merchant Adventurers	Carved chair	1940
York	Yorks.N	Methodist Fellowship Club	Tablet	1948
York	Yorks.N	Mill Mount school	Table, chairs, reading desk	1935
York	Yorks.N	Millington church	Kneelers	1943
York	Yorks.N	Minster, St Peter	Consistory court	1937-38
York	Yorks.N	Minster, St Peter	Crozier, notice board	1941-47
York	Yorks.N	Minster, St Peter	Bates memorial credence table, KOYLI	1944-47
York	Yorks.N	Minster, St Peter	Zouche chapel sanc. chair	1935
York	Yorks.N	Minster, St Peter	Clergy stalls & archbishop's chair	1942
York	Yorks.N	Minster, St Peter	Servers' seats, dias, sacrarium seat	1943
York	Yorks.N	Minster, St Peter	Lady chapel seats, desks	1945
York	Yorks.N	Minster, St Peter	St Stephen's chapel desks, seats	1946
York	Yorks.N	Minster, St Peter	Chantry chapel	1948-50
York	Yorks.N	Museum	Stairs	1928
York	Yorks.N	NR Mental Hospital	Riddel posts, altar rails	1948
York	Yorks.N	Nunthorpe St Mary	Altar, kneeler, desk, seat, screen, lych gate	1940-48
York	Yorks.N	Piccadilly Coffee House	Shop front	1933
York	Yorks.N	Purey Cust chapel	Tablet	1933
York	Yorks.N	Q. Anne Grammar Sch.	Head's chair, table	
York	Yorks.N	St Andrew Huntington	Churchyard memorial cross, litany desk	1942-46
York	Yorks.N	St Chad	Pulpit, chairs, font cover, alms dish, altar	1926-40
York	Yorks.N	St Clement	Various furnishings	1924-45
York	Yorks.N	St John's College	Various furnishings	1911-38
York	Yorks.N	St Lawrence	Various furnishings	1932-48
York	Yorks.N	St Luke	Altar rails	1942
York	Yorks.N	St Martin	Reredos, panelling, rails	1938
York	Yorks.N	St Mary Bishophill	Altar table	1930
York	Yorks.N	St Maurice	Carved figure for chancel screen	1923
York	Yorks.N	St Michael-le-Belfry	Lectern	1943
York	Yorks.N	St Olave	Pews, bench, tablet, desks	1936-38
York	Yorks.N	St Peter's school	Library furnishings	1929-34
York	Yorks.N	St Stephen Orphanage	Tablet	1938
York	Yorks.N	St Thomas	Litany desk, lectern	1943-44
York	Yorks.N	St William's College	15th century replica door	1935
York	Yorks.N	The Retreat	Monk's chair	1938
York	Yorks.N	Youth hostel	Overmantle for fireplace	

81